A Promise of Love

A Promise of Love

The Story of Terri Panszi and ARF, the Animal Rescue Fund

John W Carlson

ISBN 13: 9781511453578
ISBN 10: 1511453575
Library of Congress Control Number: 2015905195
CreateSpace Independent Publishing Platform
North Charleston, South Carolina

This book is dedicated to all those who find it in their hearts to help the imperiled dogs and cats of this world, creatures that want only to know and share the love of people. It is also dedicated to those pitiful creatures that, whether slinking through trash-strewn city alleyways, roaming empty fields or trying to survive yet another day in some equally barren and scary place, are still awaiting their forever homes.
Lastly, it is dedicated to Layla, my loud, pugnacious and wonderful little dachshund, who died in February of 2015, and was loved from her first moments of life to her last.

John W. Carlson

Foreword

Can one person make a difference in a cause in which he or she believes passionately? Terri Panszi is proof positive that one person can, though she goes out of her way to discount her importance in her own successful quest. Through ARF, the Animal Rescue Fund she founded in 1998, she has made a difference in the lives of countless innocent creatures that are powerless to help themselves in bleak circumstances, or turn away the cruelty that so often befalls them at the hands of humans.

As a former local newspaperman, I witnessed it often. This was not just in the sight of the lost and lonesome critters filling cages at animal shelters, the cats and especially the dogs pressing hopefully against the bars holding them inside, hoping for a loving scratch behind the ears, or even just a friendly word, when someone passed.

In certain respects, they were the lucky ones, at least compared to those animals whose stories of horrific abuse filled column inches of newsprint and our website. And then there were the stories of the castaways. Hard as it was to comprehend, on a fairly regular basis there were reports of some helpless puppy that had been tossed into a garbage can or a Dumpster, its plaintive cries luckily alerting a sympathetic passerby before the truck that would have carried it off to its doom arrived.

These stories always begged the question, how many hadn't been heard by a passerby? How many hadn't been rescued?

For many of us reading such stories, they made us furious. Indeed, when word of them got out, people lined up to adopt the poor creature in question, and rightly so. But in a week or two, that story was largely forgotten until the next such incident made headlines.

But it wasn't forgotten by Terri. Her love for these needy dogs and cats – plus the occasional lamb or pot-bellied pig – began in her childhood and never waned. When the time came that she could help them, beginning in her early teens, she risked much, emotionally and financially, to do something about it.

What is the difference between her and the rest of us? Lord knows. That's too complicated a question to answer here. But Terri, a loving woman whose sweet nature also masks an iron will when an animal's welfare is concerned, offered a possible answer, one that might be as good as any.

"I must have been a stray in a prior life," she said.

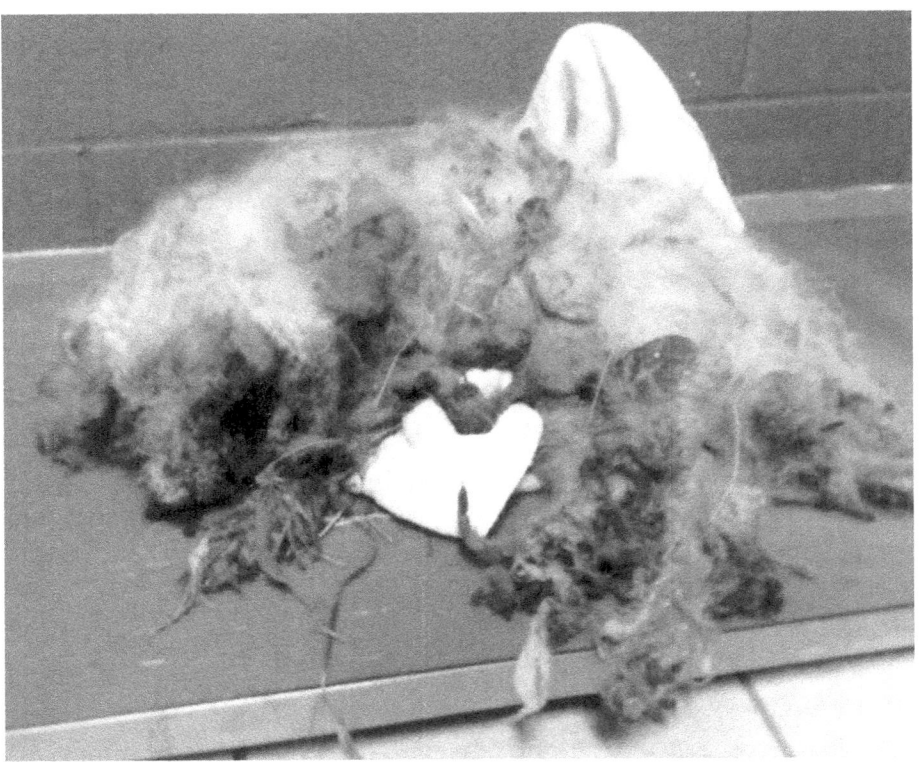

Ashley Conti, a photographer, said Arlo, "looked like a pile of trash."

Arlo

The picture, when we gathered to view it in the newsroom of The Star Press that summer morning in 2013, looked more like a thing than a being. Perhaps it was some filthy stuffing from an old discarded mattress or an ancient car seat, but surely not a dead dog, much less a live one. Its feces-encrusted gray hair, hanging obscenely like thick clumps of disgusting armor, had smelled as awful as it looked. Only by stretching the imagination, combined with intense viewing, was it possible, eventually, to make out what could be legs, a head and then, perhaps, a nose.

Looking at that sad beast, even the most hard-hearted observer had to shake his or her head and think, "My God ..."

It had turned out to be an old poodle. Found lying alongside a country road, the dog was picked up by a veteran Muncie Animal Shelter employee, and word was that employee, someone presumably used to seeing the worst that can befall an animal, had shed tears at its sight. Back at the shelter some initial efforts were made to bring a measure of relief to the dog, while word of its pitiful state spread. The Star Press' writer Robin Gibson took up its story, local radio stations followed suit, then even the Indianapolis television stations showed up to feature the sad tale. Briefly, one hoped that whoever was responsible for this travesty – and a totally heartless person that had to be – would be forced to own up to the crime, but that didn't happen. Meanwhile, the folks at the shelter recognized the severity of the animal's situation and called ARF, the Animal Rescue Fund.

Could they take in this dog?

"The second they killed the television lights, we brought him here," said Terri Panszi, her hazel eyes wet with that memory behind her horn-rimmed glasses, and her ubiquitous pink ARF T-shirt pulled over black slacks and a sweater.

As she spoke, the ARF founder was seated at the dinner table in her attractive home, a place filled with assorted Mexican and animal art. Two wide-eyed, pint-sized chihuahuas named Carlos and Pepe, both of which had been saved with extraordinary effort from black mold in their lungs, roused themselves from the comfort of a padded pillow to greet a visitor. Much like they had been, this ravaged, newfound poodle was a special case needing the kind of attention Terri could only provide at her home. With additional, painstaking trimming, the form of a dignified old dog had begun to emerge from what she called the "unrecognizable" mass of hair matted so thickly it couldn't walk or, indeed, eat. Underneath that hair were open wounds they immediately started medicating. In her own kitchen, Terri began cooking special meals for this dog. Perhaps most importantly, with her hugs, tears and soothing words, she began augmenting its memories of cruelty with memories of something it could never have foreseen from a human being - kindness.

By now, Terri had also given the dog a name – Arlo.

Why Arlo?

"He just looked like a little old man whose name should be Arlo," she explained, with a quiet laugh.

Now for the record, it must be noted that Terri has a sweet laugh that matches a sweet voice that highlights an extraordinarily sweet personality. Hers is the kind of loving disposition required to dedicate one's life to launching and maintaining an animal rescue center like ARF, one that knows virtually no limit to its care.

The watchword of her work is love.

However, she'll be the first person to tell you that deep down inside, she's not so nice. It's dogs, cats and other such creatures that are loving, kind and forgiving.

"I just wish I could be that kind of person," she said.

People who know her are apt to greet that statement with a roll of their eyes, believing she is definitely that kind of person. But the fact is, there are also people she cannot abide, people she downright despises, those being the people whose cruelty to animals creates the Arlos of this world.

"This is why," she said soberly, a finger methodically tapping a heartrending photograph taken of Arlo shortly after he was found. "This is exactly why. How could anyone do this? He is why we do what we do."

The sad fact is, the folks at ARF see no shortage of beaten, brutally mistreated dogs, cats and other pets. Terri recalled one woman and her little boy who brought in a husky puppy that had been severely beaten, plus thrown full force against a wall by the woman's boyfriend, suffering multiple broken bones. Give the woman credit, she had brought the battered and terrified puppy in. But Terri could tell she was lying about her own name and address, and that the boy had been warned to keep quiet. His tears spoke volumes, though.

"That was that little boy's puppy," Terri said.

Happily, the man who so abused that dog was later identified and arrested, but that offered only a measure of satisfaction.

"We see some of the most rotten-hearted people," Terri said, with almost a hint of disbelief. "It takes some of the heart out of you."

What gladdens the hearts of her and ARF supporters, though, is being able to help a dog like Arlo.

"He was the sweetest, gentlest soul," Terri continued, noting how once he was with her and being fed, she could help him walk in her back yard, and how he even seemed to take particular delight in walking past some beautiful purple flowers that were in bloom.

"He loved everything," she recalled. "He loved everything you did for him. You could absolutely sense his gratefulness."

Terri Panszi's kiss puts a smile on Pepe's face.

Early Days

Ask Terri Panszi about the founding of the Animal Rescue Fund, and you are struck by its place in her life. For anyone who ever waffled over where they fit in the total scheme of things, perhaps you are a little envious of her, too.

"It's what I was put on this earth to do," she said, simply, her tiny dog Carlos passed out on her left arm. "Not only is it what I love, but it's been an education for me."

She can't remember when she didn't love animals.

"I honestly think I was born with it," said Terri, whose birth in 1959, the daughter of Bruce and Nancy Gentry, made her the first of what would be three siblings. "I get animals. I don't know what it is. I admire them in their goodness."

The fact is, though, while growing up, her love of them could be trying at times, even for herself.

"I could not watch 'Lassie,' because I fretted for him all the time," she recalled, between sips of coffee from a mug bearing the message Everything Tastes Better With Dog Hair In It.

By the same token, going to movies could be nothing less than traumatic, even when they were the highlight of an occasional excursion with her beloved grandmother. The family matriarch and the kids would ride a bus downtown, stop at a diner for lunch, then go to a show, all on money the older woman had saved for the occasion. This was fine until that fateful day when "Old Yeller" came to town, and suddenly Grandma had her hands far fuller with three traumatized children than she could have imagined.

"We were screaming! We were crying! We were inconsolable!" Terri remembered, not without humor, commenting on the stir they created on the bus ride home, Old Yeller's sad fate eliciting the same sort of reaction they would also have to "Bambi."

Then Terri laughed. "I kind of thought Disney had a mean streak."

Naturally, given her overwhelming love of animals, she figured she was cut out to be a veterinarian. After graduating from Northside High School in 1977, however, there was no money for college. Instead, she trained in X-ray technology at Ball State University, work that she would undertake for 20 years. Still, she didn't wait until she had launched her career to begin the work with animals that was her true passion. At age 14 she began working at Pershing's Flower Shop, and at 16 inherited a beat-up blue Chevy that was hers, as long as she kept the tank filled with gasoline and made the insurance payments. From then until she was 35, she had a payday tradition. Cashing her check, she would take some of her money to the supermarket to buy dog and cat treats. Then she would drive to the old city animal shelter on Penn Street, pull up and honk, the signal for shelter superintendent Gayle Workman to come out and take the treats. Bringing them in herself? That was out of the question.

"I couldn't go in," Terri said, noting she was too afraid of the conditions she feared the dogs and cats were living in.

That all changed on her 35th birthday. By now the mother of two grade school-aged sons, she received a gift of $200, and knew precisely what she wanted to buy with it.

"I was going to sterilize every animal in the shelter," she said.

But with that decision also came the realization that it was time to confront her greatest fear. Even then, as it still does, the red brick building, which later became the home of the Delaware County SPCA, had the depressing look of a prison. Its border was delineated by stark link fencing, which one recent day was hung with signs warning "Keep Out" and "Private Property," its front gate secured by a length of heavy chain. But that was yet to come. For the first time in 20 years of weekly visits, she parked that day, got out of her car and stepped inside. What she saw was pretty much what she had dreaded.

Today, the memory remains fresh.

"I saw all those faces and it just broke my heart," Terri said, her voice cracking as it frequently does when she talks about animals in need, adding that today she feels guilty about not venturing inside sooner. "I let protecting my heart stand in the way of helping so many. I pacified the whole situation with a Milkbone. It does haunt me. … But that was a very powerful moment for me, personally. Enough of the prayers … enough of the excuses …"

For her, it was a true call to action. Yes, she was shocked. Nevertheless, she wasn't so traumatized that she couldn't act. Seeing that the dogs and cats in this dingy place lived on bare concrete floors, she soon bought a washer and dryer for the shelter so the animals would have clean, warm blankets to lie upon. She began bringing more food, too, and eventually worked to promote pet adoptions on a public television show called "My Best Friend," named with a nod to the music of Queen. And having waited so long to step inside the shelter, she now visited it *every* day. In doing all this and spreading the word about the place, she was also establishing contacts with people, contacts that would become vital as time passed.

Along the way, she established a good working relationship with Gayle, but one issue hung precipitously over her involvement, threatening to end it. The Muncie Animal Shelter was a kill shelter.

That issue weighed on Terri. After all, she was known to run from her workplace in Ball Memorial Hospital upon spotting a stray dog through a window, spiriting the lost animal to one of the guard shacks with a promise to retrieve it after work. Killing animals would never be all right with her, though she understood the corner that the shelter's superintendent was backed into.

"They had to do what they had to do," she grudgingly conceded.

But then her daily visits to the shelter paid off in a way she had not foreseen.

"I caught on to the rhythm of the place," Terri recalled, noting she learned to anticipate what day the shelter would euthanize animals, and even more to the point, which animals were likely to be killed.

So then? She began bringing those animals home with her, employing her personal contacts to find them "forever" homes.

By now, Terri was married to Jose Panszi, a Ball Memorial Hospital neurologist. A native of Mexico City whose mother had died when he was two years old and who had grown up dirt poor, Jose had scrimped his way through medical school. It had paid off in a successful career as a physician, work he loved, but if he thought that would automatically transfer to a carefree life on the domestic front, he had another think coming.

Among the first animals Terri brought back from the shelter were Ernie and Ellybell, two pot-bellied pigs she had set up out in the garage, something Jose discovered one evening when he returned from work.

"They were out there snorting and rooting around," she recalled, leaving unsaid what her husband's reaction to this must have been. As for other animals, in taking home those who faced early euthanasia, she concentrated on the weak and sick ones, leading to what would become a long collaboration with a popular local veterinarian, Dr. John Boyce. Meanwhile, early on she was befriended by the folks at Mid-West Metal Products, who provided her with crates and cages. She would set these up in parking lots on weekends, seeking to adopt out her rescued dogs, cats and pigs as the curious stopped to see what the fuss was about.

Still, all such efforts notwithstanding, it became apparent that her work with the Muncie Animal Shelter was not going to ultimately fulfill her goal of making a longterm difference in the lives of the animals she loved.

"It just became too hard," Terri said, reflectively. "There were no hard feelings, but I just couldn't get behind it anymore."

In the end, she left the Muncie Animal Shelter taking 13 dogs and cats she had already paid to sterilize with her, personally paying to board them at kennels. While she had no idea what it was, somehow, there had to be a better plan.

Terri outside ARF's fence, painted by artist Brian Blair.

The Birth of ARF

When Terri says establishing ARF has been an education, she isn't kidding. Unable to afford the higher education she wanted, and focused, as she was, on raising her children and caring for the animals that were her passion, there was plenty regarding the "real world" she knew little about. This was especially true as it pertained to the realistic attainment of her goals and dreams.

"I was *so* green," she admitted, almost with embarrassment. "I didn't even know what a not-for-profit was."

Fortunately, her ignorance was matched by her drive to learn.

It was a chance reading of a story in a Sunday issue of Parade magazine that began her quest. The piece was about Richard Avenzino, who had turned around a woeful animal shelter in San Francisco. Tracking him down by telephone, she had a number of talks with him, seeking advice, which undoubtedly included word on the necessity of something which Terri sorely lacked: money.

She was, however, aware of the Ball Brothers Foundation and its reputation for generosity in funding worthy charities.

For anyone who lives in central Indiana, but especially Muncie, the name Ball resonates. It was the five Ball brothers who came to town in the late 1800s to capitalize on that era's Gas Boom, starting the firm whose ubiquitous glass jars would preserve the bounty from countless gardens throughout the 20th Century, and still do. With time, the firm eventually launched into the aerospace industry, becoming a Fortune 500 company whose largesse would benefit not just its workers and investors, but students who attended Ball State University, patients at what is now known as Indiana University Health Ball Memorial Hospital, and residents of Muncie in general. Along with countless other benefits, there was also the establishment of the Minnetrista cultural center and, as already noted, the Ball Brothers Foundation. At this point, in her quest to better the lives of the area's poor dogs and cats, Terri was still hoping to work through the Muncie Animal Shelter, turning it into a showplace for the care of such creatures. Furthermore, she had arrived at a figure she anticipated could make that dream a reality.

It was $300,000.

For the casual visitor, the red-brick office building housing the Ball Brothers Foundation can be an imposing structure. A place with fine art, rich leather and the sort of desks that lend themselves to important work, it's also a place where the weight of its promises and responsibilities seem to lie heavily in the air, and the possibility of real money can be as intimidating as it is energizing. It's not hard to imagine that Terri was scared stiff as she was led to the office of Doug Bakken for her requested interview.

With thick white hair and a direct manner that promises he is not one to suffer fools gladly, Doug can seem an imposing man. Seated behind his desk, he listened while Terri made her pitch for the money, laying out the need for it and describing exactly how she would use it to improve the shelter.

Having made her presentation, she recalled, the foundation executive had one question.

"Are you finished?"

Next, she said, he told her he would not give her the money, but he would give her advice toward achieving her dream, advising her to check off a substantial list of tasks such as securing a post office box and exploring the cost of insurance.

"When you've done all that," he told her, "come back and see me."

Later that afternoon, when she returned to his office, he looked askance and perhaps slightly perturbed, until she assured him that she had done everything he asked. It seemed to make a positive impression on him. As things developed, it was the start of a close relationship with the man she now considers a trusted friend and mentor in the not-for-profit world.

"He has saved me from myself multiple times," she said, adding the foundation did give ARF a grant some time later.

Still, it left the question of how to proceed temporarily unanswered. Then her veterinarian friend, John, opened up a new clinic on Riggin Road, vacating his old Wheeling Avenue office. For Terri, whose recent education had included learning about wonderful things called grants, renting it to start her own animal rescue center suddenly seemed an obvious solution. She had even come up with a name, the Animal Rescue Fund, or ARF.

Hoping to launch it with an equally catchy telephone number, she inquired of the phone company what a special number with ARF in it would cost, was told, then decided that would be money wasted. ARF would settle for the next number that came up.

Casually informing her it was 282-2733, the phone company guy then did a double-take.

"What's the problem?" Terri asked.

"I said 282-2733," he reiterated.

"Yes?" she replied, confused.

"That's 282-ARFF," he said, amazed.

Looking back on it now, Terri noted, "It's those little things along the way that reinforce the fact that it was meant to be."

Providential as that was, however, renting the new facility was just one more in a host of expenses that were soon escalating to unmanageable levels. As medically needy dogs and cats came in, Terri was paying out of her pocket for things like x-rays and other procedures. Ever his wife's backer, the long-suffering Jose even refinanced the family home to keep ARF going, but in the end, its demise seemed just a matter of time. Obviously, the effect on Terri was telling.

"I thought, 'Oh my God, I've started something here that I can't support,'" she recalled. "I felt like I was failing."

Keep in mind that at this point in June of 1998, ARF wasn't the well known community institution it is now. Most local residents had never even heard of it, let alone knew what it did. Facing impending ruin and desperate to get the word out, one day Terri, unable to hide her feelings, walked unannounced into the newsroom of The Star Press and asked to speak to a reporter. Spending just 30 seconds with her was enough to convince anyone of her heartfelt sincerity, and what her potential failure would mean to ARF's otherwise homeless animals.

The result was a feature story about this place, one that pretty much wrote itself. It wasn't a bad feature. In fact, it turned out to be a pretty good one. Among those who read it was a Muncie businesswoman named Jackie Michael, who called Terri, whom she had never met, with a question.

"She asked, 'If I can find a place where you don't have to pay rent, will that help?'"

Yes, Terri gasped, she thought it would.

It wasn't long after that when Jackie and Terri met at a house on Riggin Road just east of where the Boyce Veterinary Clinic had been relocated. Having been vacant for three or four years, the house stood on property with outbuildings that included a barn.

"Do you think you could make this work?" Jackie asked her.

When Terri said yes, the businesswoman wrote a check for the property on the spot and handed it to the realtor.

"You just keep doing what you're doing," she told Terri.

Peppermint, The Bar Hunter

Perhaps more than anyone you've ever met, Terri Panszi appreciates dogs and cats as individuals, animals with their own ways, their own personalities, their own stories. Having noted that, some individuals are just a little more, umm, individual than others.

All of which leads us to Peppermint.

A floppy-eared, doleful-looking, black-and-white hound, the canine stranger showed up unannounced at ARF's kennel one night, obviously dropped off by some unknown someone, and was later ushered through his medical work. It wasn't until later that the dog's collar, which had come off in the process, was found bearing a tag with a telephone number engraved on it. Calling that number, Terri found herself on the line with a voice that came right out of a Tennessee holler.

"You got ol' Peppermint?" the dog's owner cried with surprise. "I been lookin' everywhere for him."

The man went on to say Peppermint was a champion bar-hunting dog, "bar" being as in the old Davy Crockett song about how he "killed him a bar, when he was only three."

You know, a bear.

Anyway, Terri went on to tell Peppermint's owner that she was calling from ARF, an animal rescue center up north in Indiana.

"How'd he get up there?" the owner asked, suddenly suspicious of what plotting had befallen his champion stud.

Terri admitted she had no idea, though she wonders now if some trucker had perhaps given the dog a lift and, deciding not to keep him, dumped him off at ARF. Whatever way Peppermint had arrived, the good news was he was now safe and sound.

The bad news was that, like all dogs taken in by ARF, he had been, uh, neutered.

"Oh, no!" his owner cried.

It was true, Terri said, consolingly, before venturing to ask if he would be coming north soon to pick up his newfound hound. When he said he had no car, Terri realized that a trip to Tennessee was in the offing and – after being assured that the de-nutted Peppermint was still wanted back home – set off south with Melissa Blair and another volunteer. Driving through the night, they headed for the Sleepy Bar Motel in Gatlinburg, where Peppermint's owner said his wife worked.

Along the way, an amazing transformation came over the hound. Where he had seemed depressed in Muncie, even before having his testicles yanked, now his spirits suddenly soared as they entered the state of his birth, with the hound sniffing the air and wagging his tail.

Balls or no balls, Peppermint knew he was heading home.

When, at last, they reached the Sleepy Bar Motel, the owner's wife proved to have a stacked beehive hairdo like Marge Simpson, but wasn't nearly so friendly as Homer's cartoon wife. Refusing to shake Terri's hand, she greeted her with, "You'd best be glad my husband isn't here, 'cause he'd punch you right in the mouth."

With that, the now Peppermint-less ARF folks headed to a nearby Waffle House for a hearty breakfast, then turned their car north toward home.

Trooper

Dogs and cats make it to ARF in all manner of ways, and one way was Trooper's. The ARF folks were going about their business one day when Indiana State Police trooper and public relations guy Rod Russell contacted them with word about a "mean dog" they were trying to capture at an interchange on I-69. Could ARF come out and help?

So it was that Terri and a longtime volunteer named Thelma Wright, a rather crusty older woman with a loving heart and a Winston cigarette dangling constantly from the corner of her mouth, answered the call. Arriving at the site, they found four state police cruisers parked, lights flashing, and the troopers mulling around nearby.

"Where's the dog?" the ARF folks asked, only to be told it was under one of the cruisers and defying all demands that it surrender peacefully.

Dropping to the pavement, Terri and Thelma took a peek under the car, then flashed the weapons they were carrying – two hot dogs. Just like that, the mean dog, which turned out to be a little gray shitzu, traded its freedom for the wieners, crawling from under the police car without protest.

"We literally had her in our arms in 30 seconds," Terri recalled.

"How did you do that?" asked the amazed troopers who, hard as it is to believe, apparently weren't issued hot dogs as standard equipment.

Anyway, shortly thereafter ARF hosted a doggy style show fundraiser at which the shitzu, who they'd named Trooper, was given an honorary

Indiana State Police badge by one of the lawmen who had been on the scene that day.

They had a good laugh recalling the day of Trooper's capture, while the real trooper admitted that all things considered, it hadn't necessarily been one of the finest moments in the annals of the Indiana State Police.

The Big Apple

As we learned from the tale of the newly neutered Peppermint, when necessary, the folks at ARF will hit the road to unite, or reunite, an animal with its forever home. That explains why in 2007 or so, Terri and Nikki Kirby got in a car and headed east. With them were a pit bull named Mabel and two cats, the surviving pets of a recently deceased Muncie man whose good friend, New York City resident Candy Heiland, had volunteered to adopt. Her city of residence wasn't the only thing interesting about Candy, who had formerly resided in Muncie. Her big-city abode was pretty interesting, too.

"It was a tiny, tiny apartment," Terri recalled, incredulously, of Candy's Manhattan place. Using one arm to cradle a sweet little dog named Lucy, with the other she illustrated the dimensions of a space not much larger than the coffee nook in which she and a visitor were seated.

What's more, reaching that small apartment required a treacherous climb up a steep, dark, claustrophobically narrow stairwell, the likes of which most of us would have never encountered, and would have found intimidating to navigate, especially with pets.

"But Candy was kind enough to say, 'I'll take his animals,'" Terri said.

Another interesting thing about Candy was her job, that being the prop director for the mega-television hit "Law and Order.'" When Terri and Nikki found their way to where they were to meet up, it was an hour before midnight outside a nondescript building, inside of which the television stars and crew were still shooting. Having been alerted to the women's arrival, a guard escorted Nikki to the set while Terri waited in the car with the animals. About 20 minutes later another guard arrived, telling Terri she should go up while he stayed with the animals. Arriving at the designated floor and stepping through a doorway, Terri was suddenly struck by a strong sense of déjà vu.

"I've seen this on TV," she thought, finding herself in the detectives' spare office and featureless interrogation room, all of it familiar save for the crewmen and cameras scattered about. Just then, she heard a man's deep voice.

"Are you Terri from Indiana?" he boomed, and she turned to encounter star Chris Noth, whose credits had also included a role in "Sex and the City."

Then, almost unbelievably, he took her hand and twirled her, singing "Terri Indiana Terri Indiana" to the tune of "Gary, Indiana" from the musical "The Music Man." Then Noth headed back off to more shooting.

Meanwhile, a disconsolate Nikki sat dejectedly nearby.

"She's sitting there, just like in a stupor," Terri recalled, laughing.

It seemed that the whole way there Nikki, who at that point was not yet married, had joked how she was going to sweep Noth off his feet and bring him back with her to Indiana. For her, too, the star of her dreams had been the first person she encountered. But when he had reached out to hug her, she was so flabbergasted she pushed him away, then couldn't believe what she had just done. Since then, when anyone had tried talking to her, she just sat there making senseless "errr" sounds.

"I think they think I'm *special*," she wailed to Terri, meaning the sort of "special" generally considered the unfortunate kind.

But with time, she got over it. The ARF women watched the rest of the shooting that night, and remained in NYC a few more days, invited to return, thanks to Candy's kindness.

"We stayed on the set," Terri happily recalled. "We ate with them. We were in. We were in. We had our badges. We just acted like we belonged."

During their stay they experienced other facets of big city life. They visited a ritzy animal rescue facility in Tribeca. They also visited Chinatown, where Terri encountered a store selling tiny painted turtles and, being Terri, wanted to buy 100 to take back to ARF, a move the now totally-recovered Nikki nixed.

"We cannot go back to Indiana with 100 turtles in the car," she told the ARF founder.

Terri had yet another big city experience one morning when, while walking Mabel a few times around the block, she encountered three guys on the stoop of a traditional NYC brownstone.

"Good morning," the homespun Hoosier said her first time around, and was answered by their silent stares.

"Nice day," she offered the second time, with the same result.

"How are you guys?" she asked the third time, at which point one of the guys said, "Where the (f-bomb) are you from? Mars? Honey, you're just too (f-bomb) nice. You don't have to say something every time you pass us."

It was a point well taken.

Still, Terri said, they weren't bad guys. But a much nicer one was encountered back on the set of "Law and Order," where star Sam Waterston proved to be as friendly a fellow as you could ever want to meet. Asking about Terri's work, he said he had a good friend who also did animal rescue work. Twenty minutes later he handed her his phone and star Glenn Close was on the line, thanking her for bringing Mabel and the cats to NYC.

As she tells this story, Terri shows you pictures of herself with Mabel, and also of herself arm-in-arm with a smiling Waterston. Then there's one of Nikki smiling broadly next to Noth, only she isn't actually next to Noth. His glassy visage is reflecting light, an image from an advertising poster hung in a subway car.

Ah, well, her look seems to be saying, maybe next time.

The Great Flood

Attached to a large piece of white poster board resting on Terri Panszi's dinner table were a number of photographs, most of them picturing people walking with dogs slung across their shoulders. Less visible in most shots was what they were walking through, but the fact is it was a couple feet of rank water. Lettering at the top of the board explained it pertained to ARF's 2011 flood, but that didn't really say much.

What it nearly was, what even Terri says it could easily have been, was the end of ARF, the drowning of her dream.

It was on a cold, wet, wintry morning that she received a call at about 6:45 informing her that there was a lot of water at ARF.

"But ARF lies low anyway," she said. "I wasn't really concerned, because I was used to standing water.

This time, though, a drainage system opposite ARF across Riggin Road had failed catastrophically, filling the animal rescue center's property with deep, murky, bone-chilling water, effectively marooning the dogs, cats and a pot-bellied pig named Chet. Soon, then-ARF director Phil Peckinpaugh was on the phone to Terri.

"He said we have to get everybody out," she recalled of his panicky call, "because we are under water."

In quick succession Terri began calling everyone she knew for assistance, and a command post was set up in Dr. John Boyce's clinic, where the Red Cross even joined the emergency services lending assistance.

Despite concerns of live electrical current in the flooded area, shivering men and women from ARF, their pants soaked and sometimes straining under the weight of their loads, were making repeated trips through the water, carrying skittish dogs and cats to safety. Someone else drove a pickup truck to a nearby Dunham's Sporting Goods store, where the folks loaned volunteers a plastic skiff to facilitate the rescue of Chet and other large animals.

"It was the most amazing thing I'd ever seen," Terri recalled of the effort, but there were more amazing sights to come.

Alerted by The Star Press website and radio broadcasts, plenty of gawkers had begun driving past to see the action. But now?

"It was unbelievable," Terri recalled. "As I looked down Riggin Road, there were cars parked all the way down on both sides."

What's more, the folks in those cars weren't all gawking; some were getting out of them to come to ARF's rescue. Particularly striking, she said, was the sight of men in business suits wading through the water, dogs and cats in their arms. Traumatizing as it was, it was a feel-good story, too, one that the Indianapolis television stations soon picked up, before the Associated Press flashed it nationwide. From his vacation place down in Florida, Terri's friend Doug Bakken later called to find out how things were going.

How did he know about it?

"You made the paper here," he told her. "Front page!"

As it turned out, all of the approximately 200 dogs and cats being cared for at the time were safely rescued and temporarily placed with foster homes, while ARF was being brought back into operation. The question was, would it be brought back for good? The stores of food and litter were gone. The veterinary supplies were gone. The stockpiled straw was gone, and none of that even addressed the damage to its buildings. ARF had faced financial troubles since its inception, but that was a known factor. Could it recover from this?

The forced evacuation left Terri reeling.

"I was taken aback at the quietness of the place without the dogs and cats,"she said with a nod of her head, mulling over that painful memory. "It was daunting. It was daunting. In my mind it was exactly like starting over. I wasn't sure we could come back. … But over time, we just started cleaning."

Happily, the same spirit that had gripped the folks who had carried the animals to safety became evident in ARF's resurrection.

"Somebody would come in and say, 'Hey, I've got some extra flooring. Hey, I've got some extra paint,'" Terri recalled. "Our community put us back together. They absolutely did. Complete strangers were so kind. We had donations from everywhere. Midwest Metal called, 'What do you need?'"

The loss of food supplies was quickly made up, too.

"Purina sent trucks," she said. "Pedigree sent trucks. Pet Smart helped."

As a response to all this, by the way, later on when a series of tornados hit Henryville, Indiana, ARF was quickly on the scene to offer assistance. Volunteers took pet food there, helped in pet search and rescue efforts and temporarily brought dogs and cats back to Muncie while recovery efforts went on in that storm-stricken town.

After what had happened to them in the flood, the ARF folks saw it as a means of payback for the help they had received, and a way to reaffirm their motto, which is, "Our Tails Have Happy Endings."

Even ARF's cats think this mug's message makes sense.

Diego

Does ARF founder Terri Panszi have a pet preference? Well, maybe, but only up to a point.

"I tend to migrate to dogs more," she confessed, with a sound-asleep Carlos the tiny chihuahua, his red collar bearing his name, passed out on her arm. "But the truth is, I love 'em all."

If you wanted proof, it was as close as the peaceful cat curled up asleep in the empty wooden fruit bowl on her dining room table. A pale but otherwise unmarked light gray, it was a handsome, good-sized

cat called Diego, so named by Jose after the legendary Mexican paint-
er Diego Rivera. The Panszis' other cat, by the way, is a female named
Frida, after Rivera's fiery and equally legendary wife, the Mexican paint-
er Frida Kahlo. At any rate, one needn't spend much time with Diego
- the cat, that is – to understand he is a privileged character in Terri's
house and life.

He didn't start out that way, though.

It was about seven years ago that Diego was dropped into Terri's
world, during the latter part of a rainy day at ARF when she was closing
up shop alone. On this day, with the skies truly pouring, she had hurried to her car and was backing it onto Riggin Road. It was then that she
noticed the bag.

This was a typical white plastic shopping bag such as you receive
from any store these days, and it had been hung from a post at ARF's
Sanctuary House. Thinking it could be a donation, she stopped her car
and grabbed the bag, which had been knotted on top. Untying the knot,
she looked inside it and …

"Two little yellow eyes were looking back at me," she recalled, noting
they belonged to a little gray kitten. Further noting how she had been
inside the ARF building when the bagged kitten was tied to the post,
she said whoever dropped it off could have easily brought it inside, but
didn't.

"That really pissed me off," Terri said.

It worked out quite nicely for Diego, however. Since she didn't want
to reopen ARF that night, she took the kitten home to care for, and
that's where he has been ever since. What's more, as if he senses Terri's
predilection for dogs, he has tried to fit right in with them.

"He thinks he's a dog," she said. "He hangs with the dogs. He loves
the dogs."

Against All Odds

Sometimes, the things animals survive to get to ARF, and then their forever homes, are nothing less than incredible. One day at the rescue center, Dean Baker, a volunteer who was also a Ball State University student, received a tragic call about a litter of Lab puppies that had been dumped in the country on a wintry day, then were struck by a car. When Dean and Terri arrived at the site, they were horrified by what they saw.

"There were dead puppies everywhere," Terri recalled.

Indeed, from a litter of a dozen puppies, apparently all but three had been killed. Hustling the survivors into the ARF van, the two then began picking up the bodies of those that had been killed. Dean was removing one the dead pups from a slushy, watery tire track when, of all things, it moved.

"Oh, Lord, it's alive!" he cried out, and soon he and Terri were wrapping it in a towel and rushing it to Dr. John Boyce's clinic, where its treatment included lots of time being warmed on heating pads.

In the final count, the three live puppies they first encountered were fine. Those that had been killed were properly buried. As for that frozen little one …

"We never dreamed that he would make it, but he did," Terri recalled of that black puppy who, based on what Dean had hollered when he found him alive, was named Lord. When he was able to be, Lord was adopted by a very nice Albany couple.

"He turned out to be a wonderful, wonderful dog," Terri said.

Lucy looks on as Terri smooches Beebee.

Lucy

Dogs just don't come cuter than Lucy. She only weighs about four pounds, with dark curly hair, an innocent face that warms your heart and two ears that flip pertly up from the top of her head whenever a sound gets her attention. She also has two dark eyes that seem to look into your soul, eyes that, for such an innocent little creature, have seen too much.

It was in 2010 when ARF received a call about a tiny dog that was running loose in the area of Colonial Crest Apartments on Muncie's west side.

In talking about her, Terri feels compelled to make a serious point: ARF is not an animal-control agency. Still, when it learns about a needy stray, its founder is inclined to act first and save complying with the job descriptions for later.

"If I know about it, I feel I ought to at least try to get it," she said, citing the dangers those poor lost creatures face from everything from coyotes and cars to people. "People are the biggest predator, sadly."

Further spurring her in this case was the fact the little dog wasn't inclined to surrender herself.

"She was very skittish and would not come to anyone," said Terri, who had long since come to realize that for whatever reason, call it an "aura" if you will, she usually had an ability to reel them in. "It's almost like they know to trust me."

True to form, when she got to the area of tangled brush and brambles where the little dog was hiding, it "puppy crawled" to her, a sorry, sorry sight. Weighing about a pound, she was absolutely skeletal, her spine and hip bones easily visible poking through her skin. Picked up by Terri, she shook uncontrollably. Despite the early efforts at ARF to feed and hydrate her, the little thing wasn't gaining weight. Naturally, this made her an immediate candidate for care at Terri's house.

"When she came here," Terri said, "she was here to stay."

It was shortly after moving to the house that Terri let the little dog into her fenced back yard. Turning away for a short time, she turned back and panicked, Lucy being nowhere in sight. Then she noticed a tiny area of fallen leaves and displaced earth. Upon closer examination, she found Lucy under it.

"She had back dug into the dirt and mulch and leaves, covering herself," Terri recalled. "That's how she had survived, hiding herself, covered with debris."

The quality of Lucy's present life notwithstanding, there is one thing about her that Terri regrets: her name. Lucy had been the name of a sick puppy that had died of Parvo, leaving behind a tiny collar, one that fit Lucy, with that name engraved on its tag.

"So she got a hand-me-down name," Terri said with a laugh. "I still feel kind of guilty about that."

It doesn't seem to have bothered Lucy, though, the sight of whom just makes you want to pick her up and hold her.

"I love her," Terri said. "I could have adopted her out a hundred times. Everyone that meets Lucy, loves Lucy."

Short Takes

- After Jackie Michael bought ARF its own property back in 1998, the first thing Terri Panszi did was get Ball State University's permission to go Dumpster diving on campus to find some of the things needed to equip it.
- By the way, despite Jackie's largesse, which also includes buying ARF its Catty Shack and more, "she has never asked for anything ever, ever, ever in return," Terri said. "I can never, never thank her enough. Without her we would not be here. She is the person who gave me my dream."
- Privatizing the Muncie Animal Shelter is one of Terri's goals.
- The key to success? "You have to learn to do all you can do, and hope for the best," said Terri, who has never taken any pay from ARF.
- Any animal adopted from ARF will be taken back if things don't work out, whether it's after a week, a year or even 10 years.
- What is ARF to the animals that live there? "It's a promise made to all of them," Terri said. "When they come in, the bad is over, and they know it, too."
- At ARF, aggression is the only thing that can cause an otherwise healthy dog to be put down, which has happened less than 30 times in its history. When it does happen, always because of the potential threat of lawsuits involving a dangerous animal, it's a veterinarian who makes the decision. "I can't make

that call," Terri said, sounding sick to even be talking about it, and noting that even then, ARF staffers are on hand for the animal's final moments of life. "Even the meanest of the mean don't leave this earth alone. They are told they are good, and that we're sorry."

- Much as Terri loves to see an ARF animal adopted by a family providing its forever home, it just about kills her to watch a car drive off with a cat or, more likely, a dog looking at her out the back window "Oh, knife to the heart," is how the admittedly emotional woman described it. She also cries when she spots someone she doesn't know wearing an ARF T-shirt or driving a car with an ARF license plate, knowing that person is a kindred spirit.

- Terri has saved the ashes of the animals that have shared her life, and wants her own mixed with theirs when she dies. She also wants some of those ashes scattered around ARF's property.

- Don't badmouth Walmart to Terri. "We haven't bought cat litter in five years thanks to them," she noted, explaining how loads of partially ripped bags keep them supplied with that necessary item, along with food and other supplies.

- She has no problem seeking help from bigwigs. "I've found that you can call and ask anybody for anything. The worst they can say is 'no.'"

- Nevertheless, she insists on running a frugal ship. "Even if we were blessed with a million dollars," she said, "operations at ARF would be the same."

- Her sons are so used to seeing new animals, she said, "If they had come home and there would have been an elephant in the living room, they wouldn't have flinched."

- Terri said she is an excellent cook, which is good news for her pets, and by default, good news for her husband, Jose. What does she cook for him? "He usually has what the dogs have," she said, laughing.

- If you ever see Terri steaming mad, you needn't wonder why. "It's always over an animal," she said. "Animal cruelty? I truly cannot wrap my head around that. The things that they endure. The things that they bounce back from, it's just amazing. They don't ever hold a grudge. Every single one of them would kiss the hand that beats them. They inspire me, their goodness. I hope it rubs off on me."
- Though she sheds tears in her efforts to rescue abused animals, that's fine with her. "It's worth those tears to try to get it to stop, and when you see them bloom, it's a feeling like no other."
- Nikki Kirby is considered ARF's "spay/neuter ninja," according to Terri. She has personally seen that more than 2,000 animals have been sterilized.
- Despite the serious business of ARF, Terri said, "We try to have fun with what we're doing." That's why at Valentine's Day the place is decked out in hearts, at Thanksgiving folks are invited to bring in leftovers for a major dog and cat feast, and at Christmas the animals are given treats and toys. Other special events held or in the planning stages include a "Fifty Shades of Grey" party aimed at adopting out gray cats, and a "Dinner Date With Wilbur the Pig" at no less ritzy a spot than the patio outside Vera Mae's Bistro, courtesy of owners Kent Shuff and Steve Fennimore.
- ARF's first animal was a tiny dog named Louise, a sweet looking little thing now memorialized in a one-and-a-half feet by three-feet photograph Terri owns. She arrived tied to a litter mate by a rope around her neck and thrown over the fence. The other puppy died. Louise lived, and was petrified of people, save for Terri and Thelma Wright. When the great flood hit ARF, Terri took her to her house and it was like, "Hello! I'm home!" She remained there, happily, until she died.
- Jose Panszi was never a rabid animal lover before he married Terri. When someone told him, "Oh, you really must love animals," he told them, "It's not so much that I love animals, but I

love Terri." Since then, he has come around to her way of thinking. "He's completely drunk the Kool-Aid," Terri said, laughing.

- Don't ask her how many dogs and cats ARF has saved, because she hasn't counted. "I'm sure it's in the thousands," she said.

- Later in this book you'll see stories about Benny and Otter, dogs whose rear legs were paralyzed, but who were made mobile by the gifts of wheeled harnesses that could be strapped to their backsides, allowing them to run using their front legs. When The Star Press ran a feature photo of a happy dog equipped with it, the author of that story and this book came up with the perfect headline: Haulin' Ass. For some reason, the editors were less enthused about that than he was.

- Phil was a feisty little chihuahua who made his home in the city police barn, back when there was a horse-mounted unit. Every now and again he'd run away, though, then wind up seated inside a now-defunct working man's bar, The Thirsty Turtle, on South Walnut Street. Terri would get a call and say, "Oh, he's there again," then go pick him up. Finally, policeman Jay Turner adopted the little guy.

- It's the rare dog that, in the end, spurns Terri's advances, but it happened once with a stray spotted roaming ARF's site back before it *was* ARF's site. Terri began stopping to feed the black and white stray, who approached closer and closer when the dog got to know her van, but could never be persuaded to get inside it. Then she learned another woman, Debbie Kizer, was feeding that dog, too. Soon the dog moved east to the site of a Christmas tree lot, where it was living in a little den it had made. Then one day Debbie called Terri, happily announcing, "I got her! I got her!" Seems when Debbie opened her car door, the dog, which she had named Baby, jumped inside and adopted *her*. "She loved her until the end," Terri said.

- As a vegetarian, Terri doesn't eat meat, but folks can't knock her as a hypocrite for using other convenient animal products, such as leather shoes and belts. She doesn't. "Think of a new line," she says, if you want to criticize her. "That's not gonna work."

- Here's an unusual ambition: "I someday hope to get arrested (for protecting animals)," Terri said. "Yeah, I would. That's my cause. That really wouldn't deter me."

- Lots of shelters don't let their dogs have treats and chew toys because of the mess they create, Terri said. At ARF, she added, "They will always, always have toys, have blankets, have chewies …" It was seeing such things at no-toy shelters, things which were collected and packed up to be donated to ARF, ironically, that cemented her resolve. She'd find a well-chewed toy, then think of it being taken away from the poor dog that had loved to play with it.

- Terri is a hugger. It's like, she can't *not* hug. Steven Smith and Brenda Bartlett, the CEO and inside sales manager at Mid-West Metal Products, a major beneficiary of ARF, enjoy their Terri-hugs. But they noted one rugged old warehouseman of theirs used to hide when he'd spot Terri, not being the hugging type.

- "I guess there are animal lovers and then there are rescuers," Terri says. "The rescuers don't give a second thought to how bloody they are, how dirty they are or what situation they are in." An example: While she admits that rats and mice tend to "creep me out," and that she has a touch of claustrophobia, when a bunch of kittens were heard mewing in a rodent-infested space beneath an old porch, she dove in to get them. Later she knew that, if she had lost an expensive shoe down there, "it would have been too bad." No way she'd have gone back in for it.

- Speaking of mice, they developed a mouse problem at the Sanctuary House once and called a dedicated pest control expert to fix it. Problem was, whenever he neared a solution, Terri would waffle, unwilling to seal the little rodents' fate. Three times he came out, and three times she called him off in the end, finally deciding to leave mouse-control to ARF's feral cats. When he died, the poor guy was buried in his pest control company uniform, and Terri worried she had overstressed him. "He was a nice man," she said, "but I couldn't let him kill my mice."

- A fellow came into ARF's office one day trying to sell a $15 bottle of cleaner to Nikki Kirby and Jane Schowe. They were going to give the persistent salesman $10 to leave when Nikki observed him slip Jane's cell phone into his pocket. Thinking quickly, she dialed Jane's number, then watched the thief fumble for the phone when his pants began ringing. He tried to explain that the pink phone with "ARF" on it was his, then fled. Nikki, meanwhile, called her husband, a city policeman.

- When it comes to animal matters, Terri prides herself on having a direct manner, but she's nothing compared to Fred Reese, at least when the issue involves housing. When the well-known local decorator visited her home in the course of adopting a puppy, he was struck by two things. "Oh my God, your house is clean!" he said with surprise, knowing the number of dogs that lived there, "but the décor makes me want to throw up."

- Terri on animal abuse: "It makes me crazy, it makes me crazy, it makes me crazy."

- An incredibly scuzzy, rough-looking fellow walked into ARF one day, dodging questions and raising concerns as he tried to adopt a little Jack Russell terrier. Terri was about to tell him to forget it, when he informed her he was an undercover cop with the Department of Natural Resources. After checking on his story and finding it to be true, she approved the adoption. Next time she saw him, he didn't look quite so intimidating, since he and his dog were wearing matching yellow and blue argyle sweaters.

- As she ages, the older Terri has a far more realistic take on the world as it relates to rescuing animals than the younger firebrand Terri had back in the day. Yet, remnants of that passionate younger woman remain. "I have yet to get it through my brain that I can't save them all," she said of the animals she loves. "I don't want them to suffer. It's just with me. … It's also my greatest curse, that I love them like I do. It's always there."

- What would Muncie be like if Terri were in charge? "If I ever run for office, which I never will, it'll be on a complete animal platform. My slogan will be 'Muncie's Gone to the Dogs.' There will be fire hydrants everywhere and Bow-Wow Bistros on every corner. That's my own little city."

- Major ARF supporter Doug White, an executive with First Merchants Trust Company, on how women reacted to a cute little dog named Tucker that he and his wife, Kathy, an executive with Muncie Power Products, had: "Every female that walked in our house went straight to that little dog and went, *'Awwww.'*"

- Sometimes, potential funding sources for ARF choose not to do so, because they only help causes concentrating on people. The Whites take exception to this, though. Doug argues that having an organization like ARF in Muncie improves the quality of life for all. Kathy, meanwhile, noted a case in which ARF rescued animals from a home in which the conditions were so deplorable, authorities later returned to rescue children who had been living there.

- Where there are dogs and cats, those critters are going to have, um, accidents, but Jose said Terri deals with them without complaint. "She loves them so much, so much," he said, then laughed, adding that since he is 75, it might be good training for taking care of him a few years down the road. Then he said, nah. He doesn't think it'll happen.

- Dr. Panszi's prescription for heading off a fight brewing between a wild-eyed possum and a couple ARF animals: First, go to the fridge. Next, remove a delicious Sara Lee baked good. Finally, begin pitching pieces of that delicious Sara Lee baked good their way.

- Examples of some of the signs found in ARF's Adoption Center: The Best Things in Life Are Rescued. More Wagging, Less Barking. A Dog Loves you More Than you Love Yourself. Talk to the Paw. Paws and Enjoy Life. A Dog Wags Its Tail With Its Heart.

- ARF began taking on employees about six years ago, and if you want to work there, the first qualification necessary is this: You must have the same fervent love of animals, and the desire to help them, that Terri does. "They have to," she said of job applicants. "They have to."

- Part-time employee Denise Ross follows a practice more of us could adopt. On country walks she picks up cans to toss into ARF's collection bin. "You're doing something good for Mother Earth and doing something good for ARF."

- Cats and dogs are very different, as everyone knows, and so are their owners. "Cat people are different than dog people," Terri said. "They really are." Happily, this is more a mark of personality quirks, we think, and not a mark of what some might embrace as nasty human habits, like sniffing where they shouldn't be sniffing, or coughing up the occasional hairball.

- Terri, on choosing animals to take home: "I tend to pick the ones that nobody else would ever want. ... I don't ever tell them 'no.'"

- At an outdoor street eatery in Mexico City once, when a poor wandering dog came to Jose and Terri's table, she ordered a plate of meat, even though she is a vegetarian, and began feeding it to the hungry canine. Then, when it was gone, Terri watched it wander over to a table where a mother and her young son sat. Suddenly, the woman began angrily jabbing her fork in the dog's direction. Incensed, Terri stormed over so blindly, she didn't notice the low-hanging branch of a lemon tree in her way, which she nailed, hard, with her forehead. It knocked her glasses askew, gave her a low forehead goose-bump worthy of Frankenstein's monster and actually knocked lemons to the ground, which excited children rushed over to gather.

- Terri, on ARF's *modus operandi:* "We are really good at thinking outside the box."

- A while back, a woman made a late-night call to Terri at home, asking for her help with what she called an "animal problem." Terri informed her she could call her the next morning at ARF. Then the woman said, "Your husband is a doctor, right?" Terri said he was. "A neurologist, right?" Yes, Terri said, he is that, too. "Well, can I talk to *him*, then?" the woman asked. "I have a really bad headache." Terri said that would have to wait for the morning, as well, adding, "She truly had no idea she had overstepped her bounds."

- Terri, on relating to her rescue animals: "We have a real nice time together, my animals and I. We sing, we walk, we dance together."

- Pixie was a teacup chihuahua who fit in Terri's hand, a dog brought in by a woman who tried to tell Terri she was a little pit bull. "No way she was a pit bull," Terri said, but the little thing did have serious health issues. But however long she had, Terri decided, ARF was going to take care of her. The last time anyone checked, that little thing weighed a solid 19 pounds, and while her odd-looking eyes hinted at a time of trauma in her life, "She's like the happiest dog you ever met," Terri said. "She never has a blue moment. Happy, happy, happy. Now I think when they brought her in, she was just starving to death." By the way, DNA testing proved she did, indeed, have some pit in her.

- Speaking of chihuahuas, Terri's affection for them may be rooted in her DNA or something. She discovered this by deciding to celebrate an important occasion in her life by getting something she almost never, ever gets – a pedicure. So she walked into a nail place, where she was confronted by at least a thousand colorful polishes racked on a wall, and picked a pinkish one that immediately attracted her. Only then did she take a look at its name, which turned out to be Chihuahua Bites. "Isn't that amazing!" she said, laughing.

A Night at the Club

For a doctor's wife, Terri seems the most down-home of women. Still, there are occasions when she has to "put on the ritz," so to speak. One such event was early in her marriage to Jose, before she had actually started ARF but was already an ardent dog rescuer. This soiree was a highfalutin affair at the Delaware Country Club for physicians and their spouses, a wingding so fancy she had actually rented her dress.

"We were all gussied up and heading to the club when something in a muddy field caught my eye," Terri remembered.

For the record, this was not unusual. Over the years, she has developed a sort of radar vision for encounters with lost, neglected, abused or threatened animals, and this time she spotted a puppy.

"Stop! Stop!" she hollered at Jose, who has the procedure down pat after countless such episodes over the years.

In a flash she was out of their car, across a fence and running to the little pup that had caught her eye, her rented dress hiked up and her high heels sinking into the wet, clinging soil with every awkward, hurried step.

"My little sparkly shoes were like cement boots," she recalled.

Nevertheless, she grabbed the puppy and carried him back to their car. The two then continued on their way to the party where, as things would have it, Terri was denied admission at the door.

"They were not rude, they were very polite," she said, but they were also insistent that she be taken around back and hosed off to avoid leaving a muddy trail.

When, at last, she passed muster and was allowed inside, she made a proverbial beeline for the buffet table where, as a vegetarian, she must have made an incongruous sight, piling her plate with roast beef and ham. She also grabbed a bowl of water, telling an attendant she had a hungry puppy in her car, before heading out to feed the little fellow.

Then she came back in and lost all track of time, dancing the night away.

Just kidding, of course.

"It was a very short-lived evening for us," Terri said of the party, noting that afterward Jose commented, "I knew you loved animals, I just didn't know how *much* you loved animals."

"Would that have made a difference?" she asked her relatively new husband, who gave the question a few moments of serious thought, then went on to prove that as a husband, he's not some sort of automatic yes-man.

"Possibly," he answered.

Terri laughed at the memory of that night. "That was my coming-out party," she joked.

An ARF volunteer shares some quality time with a resident.

Potsi

Walking across ARF's icy gravel parking lot, Michael Barrett lovingly bore a little sandy-haired dog wearing a sky-blue doggy sweater emblazoned with "ARF" on its back. No special production of the Animal Rescue Fund, the sweater had been found at Walmart by Terri, who quickly snapped up every one in the store, much to a cashier's amazement.

The dog, a shitzu mix, looked perfectly comfortable in his new sweater, but the fact is, by rights, he should never have been wearing it. In fact, by rights, he should have been dead, euthanized two days earlier. The fact that, instead, he was happily snuggled in Michael's arms, was another example of the magic – and the beauty – of ARF.

Michael's wife, a Muncie banker named Gay Ellen, and another ARF volunteer, Terre Varner, had spotted the little dog on a Facebook posting from an Indianapolis animal control site, one that made note of his pending date with death. About 10 years old, the dog was believed deaf and blind. From his head back, he had been shaved of hair that had been heavily matted with fecal matter. Found outside a city store in the freezing cold, he had been discarded in a large flower pot.

With Terri's blessing, the ARF crew drove to Indy and rescued him. In light of his sad but unique discovery in the flower pot, they christened him Potsi. Now he sat in the warm cab of a visitor's pickup truck, perfectly content in Michael's arms, in whose home he was now being fostered.

Employed as an ARF pet technician, Michael and his wife had done this all before. In fact, after a busy 2014, they had agreed to take a break from fostering cats and dogs in 2015.

Then Potsi had shown up, and Michael was happy.

"I'm so glad to have given him and Alex their first kiss bombs," he said, his head shaved and chin sporting a goatee of blond hair going to gray, unselfconsciously raining kisses on the little dog's head. "Kiss bombs! Kiss bombs!"

As for Alex, it should be explained that he was the husky puppy alluded to earlier in this book, the one whose owner had terribly abused, throwing him full force against a wall, before the man's partner and their young son had brought the dog to ARF. It was the Barretts who had fostered Alex back to health, and trained him for the time when he would be placed in his forever home.

Alex was 12 weeks old when he came to ARF, and he was starving. He had three types of worms. One of his canine teeth had been knocked out. He had 27 fractures in his ribs. His right front leg was broken in three places, breaks that the man who had inflicted all this pain tried to remedy, or more likely hide, by cutting a splint from an outdated license plate and bending it around the leg. In removing it, Michael had sliced open his hand on the jaggedly cut metal.

"I don't know how Alex didn't rip his leg up with that thing on it," he said.

Yet from the start, despite the hell he had been subjected to, Alex had trusted Michael and bonded with him, calmly letting him remove the plate.

"I just knew then he was going to be fine," Michael said. "I knew then, his perfect home was out there."

The first night Alex was with the Barretts, Michael fed him and learned a lesson.

"That first chicken strip, he liked to took my finger off," he recalled. "He was food aggressive."

Knowing that wouldn't bode well for the dog's future in his adoptive home, Michael began correcting the behavior, offering Alex chicken strips, then taking them back, then feeding them to him, all the while reinforcing the fact that he was going to get that food eventually. Then Michael began holding the chicken strips in his mouth, training Alex to remove them gently.

"I put in a lot of effort," he said, "because I wanted him to go to one more home for the rest of his life."

Indeed, Alex did end up in his perfect forever home, going to a loving Yorktown family after a search of volunteer adopters that ranged as far away as out-of-state. The new home was a place where Alex's little boy, a nine-year-old kid, even naps in his crate with him. As for Michael, when he goes over to visit, the dog he saved won't even let him take his coat off, happily jumping all over him, then insisting on being carried around, though he now weighs a solid 60 pounds.

Obviously, Michael has a special way with dogs, but it's a way that was born of immense pain.

A Selma native, he spent 25 years working in Marsh warehousing and trucking, near the end of that time injuring his back, before the sale of that business cost him his job, his pension and his potential for retirement. Still, for a man who has faced trials like that, he has a well centered sense of himself, one that emphasizes helping others.

"An extraordinary person to me," he said, "is someone who puts faith and compassion into an extraordinary amount of effort for somebody else's well being."

Or, as the case may be, some dog's.

The father of two children, Michael would take his son Brandon on regular "guys nights out," when they would grab dinner and maybe see a movie. Then, to cap off their evening, they would always go buy a 50-pound bag of dog food, tape a $20 bill to it and drop it off at ARF, a place both of them loved.

Looking back on those days now, Michael, who earned a bachelor's degree in finance from BSU in 2000, catalogs the ways he was blessed back then, including making a decent wage, having good insurance, plus a loving wife and, with Brandon and his daughter, Brittany, two great kids.

"I knew, at that point," he said, reflectively, "that I was a wealthy man."

And then, Brandon died.

The boy was a 15-year-old freshman at Wapahani High School when his parents planned a quick overnight visit to a lake cabin they owned. Brandon asked if he could stay home. After consideration, noting their son had always made good grades and shown good judgment, Michael and Gay Ellen allowed him to do so. Once they left, however, Brandon found a set of their keys and went for a joy ride in the country. When a dog ran into the road he swerved to avoid it and struck a small tree, little more than a sapling, really. But somehow, freakishly, when the vehicle struck the tree, the impact bent its trunk, which then whipped back and struck Brandon in the head through the driver's side window, killing him. Later, they were told that investigators had never seen so little damage to a vehicle involved in a fatal accident.

Recounting the story, Michael didn't cry, but just sat stroking the dog in his arms. His words, though, conveyed the full measure of his grief.

"My wife and I just had a difficult time making things fit," he said, staring out the pickup truck's front window. "My health declined. So many people don't understand. After a while, people expect you to move on … but there's no normal progression to losing a child. We were broken, and lost, and completely without love after we lost our son."

In a very real way, he said, they were like the poor dogs and cats that ARF takes in. But it was volunteering there and later hiring on to help those broken animals, work that he initially pursued to put his injured back to use again, that gradually brought the Barretts their greatest measure of healing.

Having told Terri, "It healed us as much as we could be healed," the work is something to which Michael has given a great deal of thought.

"I think everybody has a part and a place," he said, "and if you can find your way, if you can find your authentic self, you'll be a happy person. … I think we can empathize more with the animals, to help give them a second chance at life, because of what we've been through."

That Potsi was now enjoying the resultant love, two days after he was to have been destroyed, was obvious. The little dog had already put on some weight. His supposed blindness and deafness had been corrected, too, the former by removing the ear wax and ear mites that had fully clogged his ear passages, the latter by the thrice-daily application of eye drops that Michael was now carefully administering.

"He's pretty amazing," the ARF employee said of his new friend, and smiled. "He's still got a lot of life in him."

Part of Michael, meanwhile, was looking forward to finding Potsi his forever home.

"There are rare times when you get the perfect dog in the perfect home," he said. "When you see that dog's face light up, and that owner's face light up at the same time, you get to change that person's life. You're fulfilling a part of them that they had no idea they needed."

Having that sort of impact on a dog's life and a person's life, he added, was a joy that no amount of pay can buy.

Of course, another part of Michael wasn't looking forward to that. He admitted with a laugh that he and Gay Ellen had failings as a foster family, since they always ended up wanting to keep their four-legged charges themselves. Plainly, the sweet little dog in his arms had already captured his heart.

However things worked out, though, it boded well for Potsi.

"I tell you what, man," Michael vowed, "he's going to have a good life."

Tank and Angel

Can puppies paint? They can if you're referring to Tank and Angel. The proof was in a photograph framed and resting on Terri's kitchen table. In it, the two black pups were spreading colorful swaths of paw-patterned paint across a canvas laid on her kitchen floor, creating a work that was going to be auctioned at a fundraiser for Gallery 308.

The work? The style? The oeuvre?

It looked something like the abstract impressionism of Willem De Kooning.

At any rate, this was pretty good stuff for a couple of Lab-mix puppies from a litter of six or seven that had been found in a box under a porch in Anderson when they were only about five days old. Volunteer Nikki Kirby had taken the pups home, then put out a plea for a lactating mother, which was answered by a woman working as a dogcatcher in Alexandria. Soon the stand-in Mom, whose name was Macy, was feeding the pups, but with one exception.

She kept pushing Tank away.

Informed of this, Terri put Tank where she always puts pups in such cases – in her bra.

"I put them in there so they can hear my heart and be warm," she said, holding a mug of coffee bearing a takeoff on that famous line from the movie "Jerry Maquire," namely, "You had me at 'woof.'"

By that point, things were looking bleak for Tank, who was making a noise Terri calls "the death cry," a soft moan accompanied by the sort of movement a fish's mouth makes as it breathes. Nevertheless, she rushed Tank off to Dr. Christine Litt, a partner in Dr. John Boyce's veterinary clinic, who undertook some last-ditch treatment, with a result that neither she or Terri expected.

"By golly," the ARF founder exclaimed, "the death cry stopped. Tanky made it!"

By the way, so taken was she with these pups, she began blogging, not about them, per se, but for them, in their persona, detailing their daily activities and such. Here again, Tank proved to be extraordinary.

"It was insane," Terri said, happily, of the followers who fell in love with the pups by reading the blog. They loved them so much, in fact, that the reaction was equally strong when it was time to put them up for adoption, which would mark the end of their blogging careers.

"Oh," the reaction was, "you can't find homes for them!"

But Terri could and, happily, did.

Unhappy Customers

Spend any time at all around ARF and you are going to see a lot of happy, devoted, loving people. That kind of makes the rare jerks stand out.

Terri has encountered her share, but the one she most easily recalls approached her while she was helping unload bags of dog food from a trailer. If you need the help, ARF will give you dog or cat food, the condition being that after your first three bags, you must prove the dog or cat you are taking it for has been neutered.

Anyway, the fellow in question drove onto the lot in a very nice Humvee, walked over to her "dressed to the nines," as Terri put it, brusquely demanded his dog food then, when reminded about the neutering requirement, mouthed off something inappropriate.

Then, to add insult to injury, his final word to Terri was, "bitch."

To hear her tell it, she nearly flew out of that truck trailer to get in his face, something it is hard to imagine of her, but also something she does if she is really ticked off, and banned him from ARF's property for good.

Anyway, make a note: If you ever use the word "bitch" at ARF, you'd better be talking about one of the dogs. And another thing, come to think of it. If you ever have a problem with Terri or ARF, don't get in her face and tell her you're going to "take it downtown," meaning take it up with the mayor or somebody.

"Downtown's nothing to us," Terri promised.

There was an incident when one such dissatisfied customer, a big burly guy, "got all puffy," threatened to "take it downtown," then, when Terri rather pointedly responded, delivered the magic words: "I'm gonna kick your ass."

Now, truth be told, in her natural state, Terri is the least threatening of women. But what if she's angry over somebody's animal-welfare issue? That's a different matter entirely. When this guy got up in her face, she got up in his face even further, sincerely warning him, "I'll take you *down*. It may take me five hours, but I'll do it. I don't back down to that. All it does is make me mad."

Sure enough, properly chastised, this moron left with his proverbial tail between his legs.

Another time, though, Terri inadvertently earned some people's wrath via social media, and decided to live with it.

It was summer, and a little yellow terrier had been running lose near I-69's interchange at Gas City. Grabbing leashes and armed with hot-dogs, she and Nikki drove up and spotted the lost little thing, but were unsuccessful in grabbing it. Realizing the dog was not going to give in, they drove to Marion, returning with a live trap and a bag of hamburg-ers, then sat by to wait out the standoff.

"We honestly stayed there all day, trying," Terri recalled, noting they finally left the burger-loaded trap set, asking someone in a neighboring business to keep an eye on it and call when the little dog ventured inside for a bite. Eventually it did, and they returned to the interchange to fetch the dog home to ARF. Later, on ARF's Facebook page, they posted the story and the now safe dog's name - Cracker.

"We named her Cracker because she had been there by the Cracker Barrel restaurant,"

Terri explained.

The result?

"We really caught hell for that," she said, with most folks figuring that was some sort of regional slur. "'How dare you name her Cracker?' Facebook people sure let me know."

So, how did things work out? This time, Terri backed down, in a manner of speaking.

"We changed her name to Ritzy Cracker," she explained with a laugh, noting you can't win 'em all.

Beebee has a taste for the finer cuts of beef.

Guess What's Not for Dinner?

As you may have surmised from reading this book's Short Takes section, it's a darned good thing Terri Panszi cooks human food for her animals, because that's what her husband Jose usually gets for supper, too.

But not always.

"Sometimes," Terri said, "he gets something special."

Indeed, it was one of those days when she learned of tenderloin being on sale at an Indianapolis market and went down there, dropping $80 on a grass-fed cut of prime beef she indicated looked big as a base-ball bat.

As soon as she entered her home bearing the beef, of course, her two biggest dogs, Beebee and Anna, took an immediate interest in what she was carrying. Not that you could blame them, of course. After all, Beebee, a Lab/shepherd mix, had been found as a puppy in a trash toter in a Walmart parking lot, not a place where dogs typically encounter a lot of beef tenderloins. Anna, a Lab/sharpei mix, had known a rough life early on, too, coming to ARF as a five-week-old with a Parvo virus, before being healed and matched up as a playmate with Beebee.

Anyhow, after warning the two dogs that the tenderloin was strictly Jose's, Terri began cutting her husband's newfound bounty of beef into steaks before a phone call momentarily removed her from the kitchen. Upon her immediate return, however, it was like Penn and Teller had snuck in to perform their famous "Disappearing Tenderloin Trick."

So quickly had this generous hunk of meat disappeared, her first thought was that she had stuck it in the fridge. Her second thought, after checking the fridge, was to begin hollering "No! Nonononono!!!!" Her third thought was to rush along the now-obvious trail of bloody juices swathed across the floor to where Beebee and Anna were happily dining like kings.

"Of course, they were very satisfied," Terri said.

What she did next was rush over to Lahody Meats and buy Jose something really nice for dinner, though even she admits it wasn't quite as nice as an $80 tenderloin.

Healing Power

Though she doesn't claim to be a writer, Terri Panszi offers this wonderful description of a woman she knew who was severely depressed.

"She just looked like rain," the ARF founder recalled of the woman, who came as a volunteer, maybe at someody's recommendation, or perhaps to try and answer a need that she somehow recognized deep within herself.

Just walking through the door had no positive effect, though.

"Her heart just wasn't there," Terri said, recalling the woman's regular disheveled appearance, woeful persona and overriding air of sadness. "But, she kept coming back."

That's why the woman was volunteering the day Zoey, a little Yorkie mix, was brought in. Just like that, the two seemed to bond.

"It was like a switch got flipped," Terri said, noting the woman asked hesitatingly, hopefully, if she could possibly adopt the little dog. "It was like she had turned, she was headed toward something better."

Three weeks later, the woman returned to ARF with Zoey, and Terri said everyone there was astonished.

"You would not have recognized this woman," she said, her voice reflecting the amazement she felt that day. No longer unkempt, she was nicely dressed and groomed, wearing makeup and, more to the point, happy. The reason, she said, was Zoey.

"I have something to live for," the woman told them. "I have a friend to the end. It's a new life."

"It was," Terri said, "a beautiful thing to see."

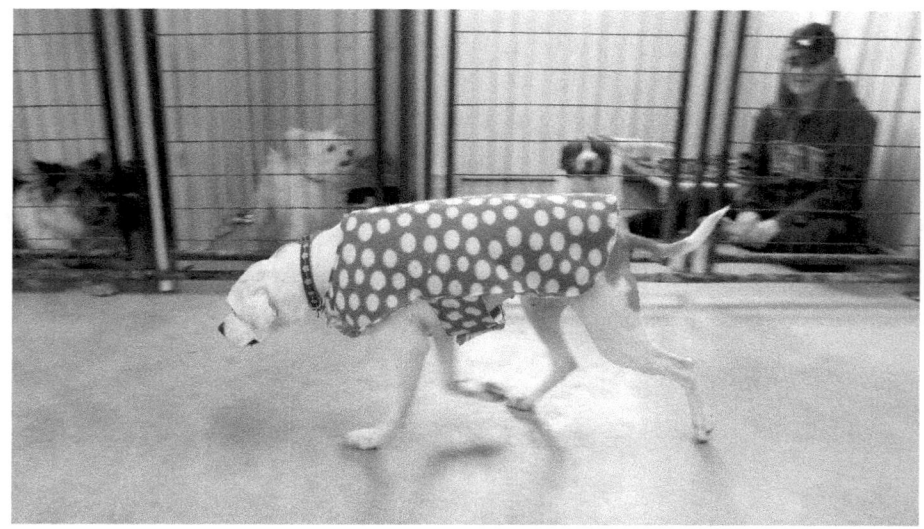

An ARF dog goes for a stroll in the Adoption Center.

Penelope

Some of the animals that pass through ARF on their way to forever homes become legends, and one of them was Penelope.

Why? She was hell on wheels, for one thing, or at the very least, hell on paws, not that anyone could blame her.

"We're talking about a train wreck of a little dog," Terri said of the tiny chihuahua. "She had every infection known to man. She became my go-to girl for decrepit chihuahuas. But she was *our* train wreck of a chihuahua."

Despite the little dog's feisty nature, to a great extent, Penelope's tale is a love story, one between her and the woman who saved her, Kristy Nacrelli.

Now retired as a kindergarten teacher for Muncie Community Schools, in the summer of 2000 Kristy was a woman with an untested determination to help the creatures at ARF. Today, the true measure of her dedication and devotion is that since then, 27 ARF animals have come through her doors. What's more, these have been rescue animals that most other folks would turn their backs on.

"We do the old, the icky and the gross," Kristy said with a warm laugh. "The ones that aren't going to make it anywhere else."

Some of those 27 have lived with her for years. Some of them have succumbed to their earlier mistreatment in a week. Either way, they all have had one thing in common.

"They have a really good end," Kristy promised.

Penelope was the first of those 27 animals, surrendered by someone who didn't want her.

"She was the most pitiful thing you could ever lay eyes on," Kristy recalled of the dog whose ears were terribly infected, whose hair was largely gone due to horrific mange and whose skin was scarred by cigarette burns. Initially kept alone in a trailer at ARF, separated from the other dogs because of her temper, she met Kristy and it was love at first sight.

"I don't know what it was, but we just clicked,"the former teacher recalled, noting it wasn't until after several months of treatment that she could finally take Penelope home. Feeding her chicken, pancakes, oatmeal and her famous buttered noodles, she noted Penelope was, "as sweet as could be with a couple of us. She loved Terri."

There were plenty of others she wouldn't tolerate, however, even including one of Kristy's sons, to whom the little dog took an instant dislike. Almost from the start, Penelope staked out her special place on the couch under pillows and a blanket, and woe to the hapless person who lifted them off, or worse, accidentally sat on her.

"She came out like a moray eel," Kristy recalled, with a memorable allusion. "She left her mark on whoever she met."

In the end, however, Penelope spent 10 years in Kristy's home, and though she was ailing throughout her life, that dog the ARF folks thought was near death when brought in lived for 17 or 18 years. When she died, it was in Kristy's arms.

"Penelope was so peaceful," she said of her final moments. "She was as peaceful as could be."

Looking back on her life, Kristy said Penelope was undeniably a character, the equal of a couple other memorable "all-stars" she has taken in over the years. What finally comes to mind when she ponders that tiny little firecracker of a dog?

"If I could sum her up," Kristy said, "for most people, she dared them to love her. For me, it was instant."

President of the Board

When Lisa Marsh talks about "my babies," you know she is talking about the four-legged ones who have come under the love and care of ARF, of which, after a long stint as a volunteer, she now presides over its board of directors.

It's a position in which she is seemingly well placed.

"I could never, *never* not be a part of ARF," said the 34-year veteran Central High School faculty member. "I love teaching, but my heart is with ARF."

A Muncie native, Delta High School and Ball State University graduate, she met Terri, who had been a classmate of her husband, Kelley, at the Muncie Animal Shelter before ARF was started. It was a meeting of like-minded women.

"I love Terri," declared Lisa, who teaches family and consumer science, nutrition and child development, using adjectives like "wonderful" and "amazing" to describe ARF. "Terri is my hero. She's a miracle worker, she really is. Without Terri, this wouldn't be a story. She downplays her role, but she has made such an impact in the lives of these animals. I am so thankful, so thankful, and proud to be a part of this big picture."

One needn't talk with Lisa long to understand why she is in her position, her determination to better the lot of animals shining through.

"My vision is, Muncie and Delaware County can become a no-kill community," she said. "I think we are moving toward that goal, but we're not moving fast enough for my liking. I want it to stop."

By that, she meant "euthanasia for space," but she is equally adamant about leaving dogs outside and dogs kept on chains.

"There's a lot more work to do," she continued, adding that ARF is just the organization to lead the way. "Our role in the community is huge, and the need is bigger. It's time for change."

To help promote that change, she often incorporates ARF and its mission into her classroom activities, and has found her students receptive to her message on animal welfare.

"Hopefully, that will have a trickle down effect," she said.

In heading ARF's board, Lisa is no figurehead. Her love of dogs runs deeply, as is evident in her own, who have come from the ranks of the sick, sad and needy ones that are less likely to be adopted than others.

"I especially have a soft spot for seniors," she said. "Everybody loves a puppy. I love puppies. But every one of our babies deserves to be a part of a family, to know what it is to be loved."

When people seeking a pet walk past the older dogs who desperately need homes, she can't take it.

"That's when my heart starts to break," she said, noting Kelley always warns her that when she takes on an aged dog, she is setting herself up for heartache. "But I'm willing to have my heart broken for them to know what it is to be part of our family."

Ask about her favorite, most poignant ARF story and she brings up the aforementioned Arlo. Indeed, after those television camera lights were turned off at the poor dog's pathetic unveiling, it was Lisa who wrapped him in a blanket and bore him into ARF's care.

Later, when another pathetic little dog came under her care – one she said was flea-bitten, blind and skeletal, with teeth she could only describe as having "the consistency of bread" – she took it home.

But what would its name be?

They settled on Marlo, a nod to Arlo.

Furthermore, they turned that poor little dog's life around.

"I truly believe that love can conquer all," Lisa said, "and what we do at ARF is a shining example."

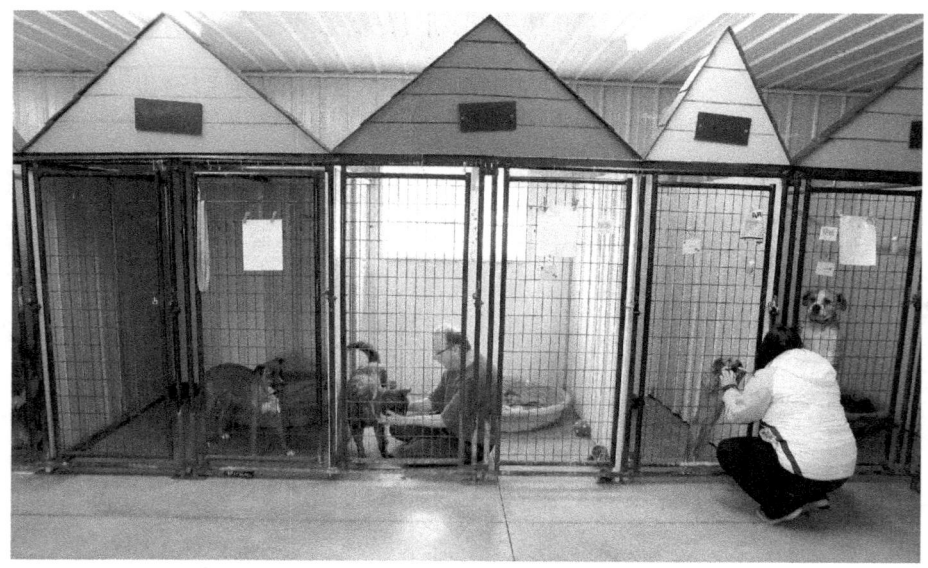

An in-kennel visit brings an ARF dog and a person together.

A Dog Named Joe

"Shelter grabbing," Terri calls it.

It's when, after being alerted to a dog, cat or multiples of the same about to be put down, ARF workers go to that shelter, obtain the animals and bring them back to a place of love, care and safety.

As a mission, it sounds so like Terri, which is why by everyone's consensus at ARF, including her own, she isn't allowed to do it anymore. The reason is illustrated by the last such mission she went on.

"We had committed to 11 dogs," she explained with a smile, "and came back with 31."

Obviously, for an organization with limited resources to house and provide for such animals, these wholesale adoptions quickly threaten to run it out of business. Were Terri to visit another shelter, however, she knows she couldn't stop herself, so it's best she just stay away.

"I can't see it, I can't see it," she said, emphatically, of the animals in line to die. "If I offer to go, my own people stop me, because I lose my mind."

That explains why it was on her last such mission that she encountered Joe, a big old lumbering black Lab/terrier mix.

"He was the sweetest dog," she recalled, sitting at her kitchen table. "Just the sweetest, sweetest dog, who did not deserve to lose his life."

When she spotted him, Joe was among the 31 dogs at Indianapolis Care and Control wearing red tags, meaning they were going to be euthanized. Naturally, Terri indicated she would take each doomed dog by "flipping its card."

"I was running through those kennels flipping cards," she said, noting she then began the process of corralling those dogs to transport back to ARF, but when she arrived where Joe had just been, her heart sank.

His cage was already empty.

"I went tearing back there," she said, taking the man who was about to kill Joe by surprise. "He was already on the table, tourniquetted. I burst through the door and yelled, 'No! He's going with me!'"

It was the closest of calls, and a few minutes later when she was in a room with the dog she had just saved, she started coming apart.

"I was kind of having a meltdown," she said.

And right then, Joe went over to where a little yellow teddy bear lay on the floor, picked it up, brought it over and laid it in her lap.

When Terri tells these stories, she is often emotional, but at this one she choked up far more. Still, she wasn't so choked up that she couldn't happily tell how back at ARF, Joe was adopted by an elderly man who, when he could no longer care for him, brought him back. Joe then lived out the rest of his life with Terri's father, Bruce Gentry.

As for the image of Joe, bringing her that little yellow teddy bear …

"That's a memory I will take to my death," she said.

Terri introduces an ARF dog to a potential adopter.

Sammy Scary

Folks who have been hereabouts a while will recall Indianapolis' scary television horror movie TV host Sammy Terry, but he had nothing on Sammy Scary, or rather Sammy the Minpin, which stands for miniature pinscher.

"This little tiny minpin was crazy with a capital C," Terri recalled, passing over two small framed photos of Sammy to help illustrate her point.

In the first, Sammy seems sane enough, kind of cute even, placidly staring at the camera with what amounts to a pleasing, innocent, doggy smile. The next photo, which was snapped just a second later? It's kind of hard to describe, really, except Sammy suddenly has a look that falls somewhere between a giant anaconda's mouthy, jaw-dropping, dinnertime gape and an imitation of Edvard Munch's legendary painting "The Scream."

Either way, it's not a pretty sight.

Of course, like so many animals who wind up at ARF, Sammy had a good reason to be crazy. The little dog had been brought into Dr. John Boyce's clinic suffering from road rash, a banged up eye and other injuries, having been thrown down a street like a football. Now, he kept jumping straight up in his cage, banging his head against the top of it with every single leap.

"He does that all the time," the veterinarian explained to Terri, of this obviously nut-case dog.

Naturally, she took Sammy home with her.

"He was the naughtiest dog I have ever had," she admitted with a laugh. "He peed. He pooped. He would poop on (her son) Tyler's bed. He barked. He bit. He spun in circles."

One time when they ordered a pizza, he latched onto the back of the Domino's guy's pants, steadfastly hanging on while the panicky delivery-man desperately tried to shake him off. That little trick put the Panszis on Domino's banned-from-deliveries list.

Escaping outside, Sammy would run, run and run some more, then collapse in a tongue-lolling heap of canine unconsciousness until Terri found him.

Sammy's most infamous act, however, has to go down in the annals of canine craziness. At the time, the Panszis lived in a house with a loft, and had engaged a workman to make improvements to a bathroom. With his work finished, he was writing up his bill when Terri noticed he seemed to be sweating profusely, to the point where it was even dripping on his paperwork.

Then, glancing up, she noticed Sammy at the edge of the loft, with one rear leg lifted.

About that time, the workman looked up, too, saw he was being peed on and hollered "Oh, my God!"

"That guy was so mad," Terri recalled. "He was *so* mad."

At one point, Terri began paying good money for weekly phone consultations with a dog psychologist, until he finally advised her to save her money. Even John her veterinarian took Terri aside and recommended euthanizing Sammy, who made office visits something to remember, or perhaps, forget. But she wouldn't do it. In the end, Sammy spent the rest of his life with the Panszis.

"He loved me, he loved me," she said of that crazy little dog. "We were thick as thieves. I cried my eyes out when he passed.

Lambies

When Terri talks about her "lambies," she practically coos the word. "Oh, my lambies," she says like a mother discussing a baby. "They opened up a whole new love for me. They made me glad I'm a vegetarian."

The newborn lambs were in Hancock County when someone at ARF spotted them for sale on Craig's List. Driving to the trailer from which they were being sold, an ARF worker who intended to buy one instead bought three, making note of the deplorable conditions at the place, which included dead lambs outside lying on the ground.

"They were a little over a week old and covered in poop," Terri said. Calling her friend Dr. Donna Wilkins, a physician with the Delaware County Health Department, she initiated the action required to have the lambs, which totaled six, along with one little billy goat named Billie, removed from the trailer.

"We put 'em in the cat house and let the games begin," Terri said, explaining how they had to be hand-fed with bottles four times a day. That was when Donna's son, Jeff, built an ingenious feeder from wood, one that significantly cut back on the work involved.

In talking about those lambs, Terri flips through a photo collection that pictures them from their first imperiled state to their arrival at ARF. They include a favorite shot by Star Press photographer Jordan Kartholl that pictures a lamb practically jumping into her outstretched arms. Others show the now-thriving lambs drinking at their feeder and generally doing what happy lambs do.

"Oh, they were such a joy!" Terri exclaimed. "They're just so love-filled, and so bonded. They traveled in a little group."

As they grew, their ARF caregivers logged their feedings on the wall alongside their names, which included Olive, Bluebell, Lambert, Clarice (fans of "The Silence of the Lambs" will get the reference), Eileen and Cupcake, which was changed when they learned he was a male, to Cupcakeman.

When, at last, it was time to leave ARF, they were taken to live out their days at the sanctuary farm of Dr. Joe and Amy Landwhere.

Even separated from Terri, though, they remain very special to her.

"They were such sweet, sweet, sweet little creatures," she said. "I know they're considered livestock, but not to me."

Otter

It's not every day you run into a dog named Otter. Nor is it every day such a dog overcomes a severe handicap, then proceeds to change your life for the better.

A golden retriever-mix puppy, the little thing had been stomped, severing his spinal cord, and was delivered to Dr. John Boyce's office - unable to walk or to control his bowels - by a man who then bolted away. It was then that the pup encountered volunteer Kathie Beals, who was a professor of nutrition at Ball State University.

"I met him when he was first brought in," she said, "and we connected right away."

Ask what Otter came to mean to her and she pauses, then chuckles, like you might as well ask why air is so good to breathe.

"He was a true love," she said after a few moments thought. "He meant the world to me. He taught me …"

Well, that would take some more thinking.

In the earlier days, Kathie, who earned her doctorate in exercise science, worked out Otter at ARF by wrapping a sheet around his hind legs. She would then hoist them off the ground as she ran alongside, with him moving solely under the power of his front legs. Fortunately for Otter, ARF had earlier been home to another paralyzed dog named Benny, a dog that the company Doggon' Wheels became interested in helping, building him a wheeled harness into which he would be strapped, allowing his immobile rear legs to roll. The owners of that company had adopted Benny. Contacted by ARF, they then sent another rig to Otter, free of charge.

Now, the company had included material noting Otter would likely be leery of the contraption to begin with, and that he should be introduced to it gradually. Kathie considered Otter's spunk and thought differently.

"I just put him right into it," she recalled of that special day. "The minute I hooked those wheels to Otter, he took off like a bullet out of a gun. It was like a total transformation. He was like a dog on a mission."

But if Otter was now mobile, Kathie was, too, as her career took her to California and then Utah. Still, that special dog was always on her mind, and she would come back to ARF to visit him twice a year.

"My friends all thought it was to visit them," she said, laughing, but it was her reunions with Otter that truly stirred her. When he heard her voice, he would loose a special bark saved just for her greetings. Finally, the time came to move Otter to her home in Utah, which she did after making it accessible to his wheeled harness.

Thinking back on that special dog now, she still sounds awestruck by him.

"He was the most amazing dog," she said. "His spirit, his joy for life were incredible."

With him weighing about 75 pounds and her tipping the scales at a mere 95, moving him in her SUV required cooperation.

"On the count of three he'd put his front legs in the car, then I'd lift his back legs in," she recalled. "What he really taught me was perseverance. He taught me acceptance. He wasn't always happy because of his physical condition, but he would find joy in every day. In my neighborhood, everybody knew Otter."

As maybe Otter's greatest gift to her, he taught her how to help Micky, another disabled dog she owned that was very, very special to her.

Indeed, she attributes the lessons she learned from Otter with helping her start her own animal rescue center, Herding Haven, which concentrates on special-needs dogs.

"I really feel like, given his disability, he had an amazing life," Kathie said.

An ARF cat peeks shyly around a corner.

Here, Kitty Kitty Kitty

Much as Terri loves cats, there are two she'd just as soon have never met.

The second cat's encounter happened rather recently, but should she ever want a reminder of it, she need only fetch the pair of stiff leather work gloves she was wearing at the time. They are heavily soiled, but that's no big deal. However, they are also pocked with tiny little holes, and those holes were made by cat teeth. There are also a couple dark red splotches, and those were made by her spilled blood.

Her adventure started with a call from Gaston, where a sweet little stray beagle that ARF eventually named Conner was being held by a woman. When she got there, though, a little black cat, also a stray, was being held, too, in a big Great Dane cage. It was hunkered down in a corner, but if the cat had a crazy air about, Terri didn't notice, at least not until she crawled into the cage with it.

"Then the cat went berserk," she recalled with an involuntary shudder. "It was like a UFC cage fight."

"Rrrrrrrrrr!!!" the maniacal cat was screeching and growling. *"Rrrrrrrrr!!!"* Meanwhile, it also had her head in a death grip and was biting her hands. What's more, the woman had latched Terri inside the cage to keep this little feline version of Cujo from escaping.

"I am winded," Terri recalled of the ensuing confrontation, "but I'm trying to maintain kindness ..."

And what is the woman who introduced her to this insane cat doing?

Standing outside the cage cooing, "Oh, it's OK. She's just afraid."

Meaning the cat.

It was a sadder, bloodier, yet wiser Terri who finally got the cat safely stuffed into a travel cage for transportation back to ARF. Speaking of which, it was shortly after she started ARF back in 1998 that her first unfortunate cat encounter occurred.

Terri was inside working when a woman with what appeared to be a significant disability – two severely stunted arms – walked in bearing a cat and kittens in a small travel cage. Examining the cage and its contents, one thought quickly came to her mind.

"I don't know how she ever wrangled these guys in there, because that cat was meaner than hell," she said, adding that it soon became obvious to her the cat, which was making some very scary noises, was also killing her kittens.

Sticking her ungloved hand into the cage, Terri immediately jerked it back out with a crazy cat attached.

"That cat bit me all the way to the bone," she said, adding she was trying not to scream. "I was trying to be Terri from ARF."

Still, she knew she was in a tight spot, one in which she could use a little assistance.

"Can you *help* me?' she pleaded with the woman.

"I can't," the woman answered. "I don't have any arms, and I'm late for work."

With that, she wheeled and headed out the door, soon to be followed by the cat that had attacked Terri.

"I knew right away that this was gonna be bad," she recalled, noting that, after soon growing sick to her stomach, she went home and consulted Jose, who advised her to take some Tylenol.

As her hand and arm turned bright red and began to swell, however, she knew she needed a doctor, an opinion that Jose now shared. In the end, she went to a clinic, then was admitted to the hospital, where she stayed a week, having her wound cleaned out, downing antibiotics and, oh yeah, receiving rabies shots.

"It wasn't bad," she said of those, despite their torturous reputation..

Anyway, the fact she wore gloves during her last cat attack is proof she learned something from the first one.

"When I deal with feral animals now, cats especially, I do wear gloves," she said, adding that she should have known things were going to be bad, "from the noises that were coming out of that carrier."

By the way, she never saw the woman with the stunted arms again.

"I'm still baffled as to how she got them all in there," Terri said of the cat and kittens. "That was something."

He's WHAT?

There was a time when Terri took a dim view of people who lost their dogs, but that was before Carlos also ended up among the missing.

Now, you must understand two things. First, at about three pounds – three "tiny, rickety pounds," as Terri describes them – Carlos epitomizes the pint-sized pooch. A determined sparrowhawk could probably carry him away. Second, though Terri loves all animals, he is quite possibly her favorite in the whole universe, and often a fixture on her arm when she sits down to talk.

So when the birth of her first grandson, this to her son Cody Panszi, took her to Colorado not long ago, her reminder to husband Jose and son Tyler Munson that they were "in charge of everybody" certainly included her beloved little chihuahua. That's why, when the little guy suddenly came up missing, the two knew they had stepped in deep, deep doo-doo. How did it happen? It seems that Terri's rule was that Carlos was never to be allowed out front, where a dip in the ground created a small space in the fence that he could crawl under. When Carlos was inadvertently let out there, that's exactly what he did.

"I think he was probably looking for me," Terri said.

For a while, Jose and Tyler thought a bump in his bedding was the little fellow. But when they discovered the bump in his bedding was just that – a bump in his bedding – and the tiny dog was actually gone, the freaked-out Jose was literally beside himself with worry. Then they received a call from the Muncie Animal Shelter, whose workers had found plucky little Carlos wandering the neighborhood. Luckily, city shelter superintendent Phil Peckinpaugh, a former ARF director, recognized the dog, locked him safely in his office and called the Panszis.

Thankfully, by the time Terri called from Colorado just to make sure everything was fine at home, Carlos was back, safe and sound. Tyler, in turn, was free to laugh with relief and tell his mother about the worrisome phone call he had been planning to make.

"He wasn't sure how he was going to tell me that a) they had lost Carlos, and b) Jose died," Terri recalled..

The aftermath? Well, Terri's friend Ann Marie Ross bought Jose a sweatshirt for Christmas with a message reading, "Who let the dogs out? I let the dogs out."

Also, the incident created a little buzz at the shelter, where some employees noted that Carlos wasn't neutered. That led Phil to explain, however, that Carlos couldn't be neutered because his health prevented him from being anesthetized.

"He can have no anesthesia ever, for anything," Terri said.

But, as noted earlier, the experience also made her think a little more sympathetically.

"So yes, Terri Panszi has had a dog end up in the animal shelter," she conceded. "That was humbling, and a good thing for me. I'd always been a bit critical; how do people lose their dogs?"

Now, thanks to Carlos, with an assist from Jose and Tyler, she knows.

Top Dogs

Back in 1998 when Terri was launching ARF, Ann Marie Ross read a newspaper article about her and, being a lifelong dog lover, too, tracked her down to make a contribution. Since then, the two women have become great friends, and Ann Marie's ARF involvement has gone way beyond the financial to the personal.

In fact, she and her husband Dave have had a number of ARF dogs, including some that were, or are, veritable legends.

Walk into their impressive home and you are soon happily accosted by Shelby and Snickers. The former, named after Carroll Shelby, the late American race car designer of whom Dave is a great admirer, is a sweet little white, gray and black guy of indeterminate origin.

The other is Snickers, who … well, let's get back to Snickers in a minute.

Other dogs here over the years have been mostly curly-haired whitish ones like Lola, who won Ann Marie's heart by resting her paws in her lap when they met on an ARF visit. She has a great outdoor photo of her with a fake squirrel held firmly in her mouth, only the squirrel turned out to be real, though decidedly dead, its bushy tail erect with rigor mortis.

"It was already stiff," Ann Marie noted, when Lola found it.

Then there is the aforementioned Trooper, so named because as a little lost stray he held off four Indiana state troopers by hiding under one's patrol car, before Terri and Thelma Wright coaxed him out with hotdogs. Ann Marie adopted him, too.

Then there was Ollie, a little white Maltese. A three-pound stray who was being held in the Sanctuary House, when Ann Marie saw him it was *ta-da* at first sight.

"I just fell in love with him," she said.

As things turned out, Ollie had chutzpah in inverse proportion to his tiny size. Ollie also had an unexplained enmity for the Rosses' landscape professional, Danny Wasson. One memorable day, Ollie and Danny wound up in the garage together, unaware of each other's presence, until suddenly, their eyes locked.

"It was like the standoff at the OK Corral," Ann Marie recalled.

Dave nodded in agreement. "As they instantly froze," he said, dead serious, "you could hear the strains of 'The Good, the Bad and the Ugly' playing in the background."

Unfortunately, Danny must have blinked first, because next thing you knew, Ollie was chasing him all over the Rosses' beautifully sculpted lawn.

Then there was Gabby, a grubby little ARF dog that, when Ann Marie groomed her, came out looking like a showstopper.

Oh, and there is no forgetting Zuzu, named after Jimmy Stewart's wild-haired daughter from "It's a Wonderful Life." Upon the dog returning home dry as a bone after being caught outside in a torrential rain storm, Dave was led to jokingly speculate she had been beamed up, then down, by a spaceship.

Hey, sounds plausible to us.

But let's get back to Snickers, who is one of ARF's most memorable dogs ever.

Sweet as can be when she greets you, you can't help but notice she is far from Ann Marie's typical curly-haired white dog. A sort of rusty brown from the tip of her tail to her dark nose, she has an adorable face that once graced one of the Ross family's Christmas cards.

Talk about your hard luck stories, though. A number of years back, Snickers was a stray who was hit by a car in the city, then was hit by another car. It was a third passing motorist who called the city animal shelter, where Terri said the injured dog lay for three days, unattended. Finally, somebody called ARF.

The poor little dog had a number of broken bones. While ARF's favorite veterinarian, Dr. John Boyce, was willing to work on her, he didn't have the proper material. Terri, however, knew a physician who did. Before long, Dr. Scott Walker provided the bolts, the backing and other material needed, then worked alongside the veterinarian to repair Snickers' broken body over three days of surgery.

How did the dog take it?

"They all said the entire time she was there, she never snapped at anybody," Ann Marie recalled. "She tried to lick everybody."

Seeing Snickers move about their place now, an observer can only marvel at what a wonderful dog she is, and what the veterinarian and the physician did for her.

"She still has a couple metal plates in her," Ann Marie said, "but she can run like a greyhound."

That makes Snickers and ARF a pretty successful pair.

"That place is just incredible," Ann Marie said. "The lengths they go to to save a dog blows my mind."

Uh, Nice Place You Got Here

Before Terri Panszi started ARF but after she had begun rescuing animals, she and Jose planned to attend a four-day conference, so they engaged the services of a pet sitter. Of course, keep in mind that they were country folks then and were housing 12 or 13 dogs, more than half of which, Terri acknowledged, "were naughty."

Anyway, off they went, but when they returned, they truly thought their home had been burgled and ransacked. Then they spotted the note from the pet sitter, which read: "I'm not sure when it all went wrong, but it did."

That was putting it mildly. Wallpaper was ripped off walls. Stuff was tossed around, torn and broken. Near the message that had been left them rested a single mauled shoe. Even the carpet was dug up and flipped over.

"It looked like a giant burrito," Terri said.

Naughty dogs, indeed.

Seeing all this, a quietly seething Jose walked to their bar and poured himself a stiff tequila. Then he poured himself a second stiff tequila. After he downed it, he said, "Well, let's clean it up."

When they were finished and the carpet yanked, Jose told Terri, "It appears you want to live in an animal shelter," then declared, "so be it."

"For nine months I had no carpet or other flooring," Terri recalled of that house, although she and the kids compensated by using the bare floor as a giant chalkboard, drawing pictures, tic-tac-toe games and more whenever they wanted.

By the time they bought new carpet, ARF was up and running, but not in their home.

To this day Terri isn't quite sure what the pet sitter was doing, but reiterated, "They *were* naughty dogs."

A Matter of Cans

ARF has been collecting pop cans as a source of funding for years, but thieves have actually stolen some, or at least tried. Once, Terri happened to be riding with her sister, Lorri, in Lorri's BMW, when she received a call about two guys in a nice, new pickup truck tossing whole bags of collected cans into its bed. Hurrying to ARF, the sisters spotted the thieves and, while Lorri quickly parked to block the exit, Terri raced to the truck, jumping into its bed among the purloined cans.

"You're not taking these cans!" she hollered, much to the men's surprise, tossing bags back out with one hand while holding onto the truck with the other as its driver fishtailed his way to freedom. Although Terri eventually fell out, and the driver managed to speed away, the sisters jotted down the truck's license plate number and called the cops.

Soon the "candits" were returned to ARF, where the cops made them throw the remaining cans back. After one of the guys protested that some of the cans were legitimately theirs, Terri told them, "Well, too bad. They're mine now. I'm taking them all."

When somebody noted that being thrown from a pickup truck bed was a good way to get seriously injured or killed, even in the act of protecting ARF's precious pop cans, Terri said, "That would be all right. We all gotta go sometime."

ARF's Nikki Kirby (left) works with volunteer Sherry Richardson.

Volunteers

Ask about ARF volunteers, and Terri says, "Well, they're wonderful, and there's a handful that are beyond wonderful."

Sherry Richardson is one who comes to mind. Head of the Sanctuary House, where some of the most challenging dogs are kept, she knows and loves every single one.

"She's amazing. She can touch every single dog in there," Terri said, noting that even she can't do that. "And she loves Chet the pig, and Chet loves her."

Cheryl Haas in the Catty Shack also comes to her mind. A quiet, loving woman, she is there nearly every single Saturday of her life. "If she's not there," Terri said, "we all go, 'Where's Cheryl?'"

Ball State University provides some great volunteers, too.

"A lot of the Ball State kids are wonderful," Terri said, between sips of coffee from a cup that read Dog Mom: A Perfect Child Has Four Legs. "There usually turn out to be about five who become just superstars."

Back when she started ARF, she noted, she had 11 or 12 volunteers that she described as "just diehard wonderful. And the more we did, the more volunteers that came. These were no-kill kind of supporters."

Yet another top volunteer is Debbie Norrick, who grooms ARF residents a couple times a week. But it's another skill in Debbie that Terri holds most dear: That's her ability to befriend "backyard" dog breeders, the sort that the ARF founder, who is not one to mince words, calls "godforsaken breeders that are just soulless."

While she says some breeders are OK, she is referring to the puppy mill ones who breed their dogs until they are nearly dead and suffering from pyrometria, an infection of the uterus.

"I'm damning the backyard breeders, the ones that do it as a money source, who view the dogs as a commodity," Terri said. "It's wrong; it should be illegal in my opinion."

What's more, Terri said, they often breed the runts of the litters of Yorkies and Malteses and such, angling to get smaller and smaller dogs because they look so cute and sell better.

But while many such breeders kill their dogs when they are of no further use, Debbie has gotten to where some will call her instead of putting them down, or sometimes even sell them to her to take to ARF.

For that, Terri is grateful, because she could never do it herself.

"I admire that she can even look those people in the eye," she said.

With Friends Like That ...

When an animal's welfare is concerned, Terri isn't afraid of who she must confront to get it to safety. For example, a number of years back, the Muncie Animal Shelter had a husky named Maya with a litter of 13 puppies which, for reasons she never understood, were going to be put down.

ARF sent Nikki, who was a BSU student at the time, to fetch them all, but she was told ARF couldn't have them.

Upon hearing this, Terri informed the shelter folks that if they refused to turn the dogs over and went ahead with their plans to euthanize them, she'd be on the phone to The Star Press and the Indianapolis TV stations quicker than it takes a Saint Bernard to chomp a Dog Yummy.

"It's going to be a busy media day for you," she warned.

"Well, send Nikki back over," the shelter folks conceded.

An even more surprising confrontation occurred right before Terri started ARF, when she was still hoping to make major improvements to the city shelter. With a group of others, including shelter superintendent Gayle Workman, she toured the Indianapolis Humane Society facility to get some ideas. It was a nice place, Terri recalled, and when she walked past a cage holding a large shepherd mix named Misty, who put her paw through the bars for a touch, she touched the dog back and soothingly said, "Oh, you'll get a home quickly."

Then she noticed Misty's red tag, asked the woman leading the tour what it meant, and was told that because the dog was five years old and big, it was going to be euthanized.

"Well, I'll take her," Terri immediately offered, and was told it was too late, since Misty had already been "processed."

This was not what Terri wanted to hear.

"Well, I'm not leaving here without her," she said.

Before long, her tour companions were growing a bit antsy over the brewing standoff. Still, Terri refused to leave, demanding to talk with the shelter's director, who also informed her that Misty had been processed and it would take an executive board meeting to reverse things.

Well, you'd better get started, she told him, threatening to call the Indianapolis TV stations should anything unfortunate happen to Misty.

The next day, Terri called every hour on the hour to check on Misty's progress. The day after that, the director got on the phone and said, "Come and get her. Just come and get her."

Terri did, and soon put Misty in a loving home.

By the way, she is sure things have changed significantly down there since then. But another thing that really bothered her there was the euthanasia room, which was decorated in a bright and flowery fashion, as if that would ease some poor dog's final moments.

"I remember thinking, what a crock of crap," Terri recalled. "There's no amount of art that can make you feel better about taking the lives of these animals. That little smiley-face tulip over there? It ain't working."

Bad Jose, Good Jose

Once upon a time, ARF had a Capuchin monkey, and Terri wanted him. Wanted him badly, in fact. The reason she wanted him – J.J. was his name – was that she adored him.

"He was an owner surrender," she recalled, wistfully. "He was 15 years old, and had spent most of that time in a cage. And he was so smart!"

For example, Terri had given him a little purse, and he'd carry things around in it, and take things out of it, then put other things back in it. What's more, it turned out he was a skilled artist, or at least a determined artist, taking crayons and markers to paper whenever he got the chance.

"And when he was done, he'd get another piece of paper!" she gushed.

So, Terri wanted J.J. to be kept at their house, but Jose turned a deaf ear to her pleas. What's more, he still turned her down when she offered the deal she thought would surely make him come to his senses: She'd dress them both, Jose and J.J., in matching outfits!

Wouldn't that be fun?! Would't that be the height of cool?!

To this offer, he turned to her with a look of disbelief.

"Terri, have you lost your *mind*?" he cried. "No monkey!"

"He sounded just like Ricky Ricardo," Terri recalled of that day. "It was an absolutely 'I Love Lucy' moment. … I still hope to have a monkey some day."

By the way, in Terri's mind, countering this painful spousal rejection, was the time the folks from Second Harvest Food Bank called to say they had a semi-trailer full of wet pet food that they weren't allowed to give away. Would cash-strapped ARF want it? Yes, we would, Terri told them. Trouble was, ARF would have to come up with $2,000 to cover transportation expenses.

So Jose paid the $2,000 for Terri as a Mother's Day gift.

"It was the best gift ever," she said with a smile.

A Dog's Will

*This is something ARF hands out to
visitors and adoptive families.*

Before humans die, they write their last Will & Testament, give their home and all they have, to those they leave behind. If, with my paws, I could do the same, this is what I'd ask …

To a poor and lonely stray I'd give:
- My happy home.
- My bowl & cozy bed, soft pillows and all my toys.
- The lap, which I loved so much.
- The hand that stroked my fur & the sweet voice which spoke my name.

I'd will to the sad, scared shelter dog, the place I had in my human's loving heart, of which there seemed no bounds.

So, when I die, please do not say, "I will never have a pet again, for the loss and pain is more than I can stand."

A Promise of Love

Instead, go find an unloved dog, one whose life has held no joy or hope and give MY place to HIM.

This is the only thing I can give ... the love I left behind.
Author Unknown

ARF's Jane Schowe delivers food to the Adoption Center.

Dog Woman

You can call Jane Schowe "dog woman" and the co-director of ARF won't be offended.

"I do all things dog," said the retired Muncie elementary school teacher, who started as a volunteer seven years ago before joining the staff. "It was not in my scheme of things for retirement."

But that's how things worked out.

A lifelong animal lover, the quick-laughing woman with short gray hair was at first hesitant to become involved with ARF, for one very good reason.

"I was afraid I'd bring everybody home," she said, "which turned out to be the case."

Her involvement began when, under the program "Pounds for Hounds," she began walking ARF dogs with her friend Kristi Nacrelli. That, as the saying goes, was pretty much that.

"You just get hooked real easy, and that's what happened to me," said Jane, whose stops on the way to ARF's co-directorship have included being a cleaner and then adoption coordinator, a post in which her people skills and record-keeping skills from school teaching days have undoubtedly paid off.

Along with her other duties, she also loves to foster dogs, and says her own are used to an endless stream of fellow canines coming into and going out of their home.

As for the permanent dogs in her life, they have included an interesting bunch, starting with a little chihuahua she assured her husband, Jim, was only coming to their home to die, which it did, nine years after arriving.

Then there was the schnauzer, Mr. Puck, who, suffering from pneumonia, also came to their home to die, six years after arriving. An interesting thing about Mr. Puck was, after being nursed back to health by Jane, he started acting like a jerk toward her.

"He didn't like me," she recalled, laughing but clearly mystified. "I saved his life and he treated me like that. Once he got better, he was done with me. If I'd bump into him, I'd have to run."

Even as she told all this, however, she noted that Mr. Puck had stayed in their home until the very end.

And then there is Jim's favorite, Trudy, a little sweetie they saved from Parvo.

"She loves my husband," Jane said, noting the feeling is definitely mutual. "When he comes in and says, 'Where's my pretty girl?' he's not talking to me."

Finally, there is Charlie the husky, a dog they adopted for protection from burglars after their small dogs once welcomed such an outlaw into their home. Problem is, as a guard dog, Charlie is more of a chicken.

"He would tell them, 'Come on in!' I'll show you where the valuable stuff is," Jane joked.

Still, she loves all the dogs they encounter, even though she started off at ARF as more of a cat person.

"I do sneak one home every now and then," she admitted, but that's OK for a woman of her commitment. "I'll be here for as long as I can, and maybe beyond. You get hooked on these guys."

Can Man

You probably remember from a few pages earlier that, when confronted with pop can thieves, Terri risked her health to get them back, cans being an integral part of ARF's funding plan. The man she credits with starting the effort, though, is Bob Cunningham Jr.

If that name sounds familiar to Muncie-area residents, it's because Bob's late father – Bob Cunningham Sr. – was once Muncie's mayor. A Democrat and populist in the best sense of the word, Bob was a down-home guy, a former small-store grocer who drank his Budweiser on the rocks, for crying out loud. He was also as nice as the day is long and a true gentleman, a man whose only goal was to help his constituents.

A lot of that rubbed off on his son.

Bob Jr. made Terri's acquaintance back when ARF was on Wheeling Avenue. Looking for a dog to adopt, he walked in, found her caring for one and was instantly impressed.

"She had been up all night with a sick animal," he recalled, adding that fact made her someone he could believe in.

While some people had donated cans to ARF before, it was Bob who spearheaded cashing them in and bringing the money to Terri, a helping hand she appreciated at ARF'S outset.

"She gave me a shirt that said 'Can Man,'" Bob Jr. recalled. "She's one in a million. My wife Roberta and I think the same thing about her husband, too."

When he left Terri after their first encounter, he adopted two dogs from ARF, one of whom – Murphy – became his soul dog.

"He was like my shadow," Bob Jr. said. "Some people thought he was a wolf. He had a wolf's head, a coyote's legs and a chow's tail."

These days, he thinks about Murphy a lot, perhaps especially when he visits the shrine he built in his backyard in the dog's honor, a place that includes a cross and a prayer station where you can kneel and commune with the spirit world. Obviously, he is one of the people whose life has been deeply touched by Terri, something he finds a little mind-boggling.

"With every animal that she has had adopted," Bob Jr. said, "she has touched somebody."

Friends in High Places

Drive up to Mid-West Metal Products' gigantic facility on Muncie's south side and you are struck by one thought: Wow, this place is huge.

When CEO Steven Smith comes out to greet you in the lobby, you are struck by a similar thought, that being: Wow, this guy is tall.

But he's also downright friendly, a trait he shares with Brenda Bartlett, a woman of considerably shorter stature than his, and Mid-West Metal Product's inside sales manager. Regardless of their height or lack thereof, both are giants to Terri and ARF.

When Mid-West Metal's supplies of crates and the pet cages it sells are deemed obsolete, some of them are donated to the Muncie Animal Shelter and other shelters nearby, but the vast majority are given to ARF. The reason is that they hold Terri in such high esteem.

"She's the main show," Steven joked. "We're Sideshow Bob."

"We know ARF's a clean shelter," Brenda added, "and very well organized."

This makes Mid-West Metal, and by extension, Steven and Brenda, VIPs to ARF. But even Steven acknowledged that if they are talking to ARF folks and what looks like a stray dog walks past, that dog is going to take priority.

As a rule, the company's largesse is extended to ARF twice a year when, say, they have added a new product line and can't sell out of the old. ARF also benefits when samples come in from vendors.

"We're constantly getting samples in," Steven said.

One good thing Terri does to avail herself of their help?

"If she needs something, she'll pick up the phone and call," Brenda said, alluding to one of the lessons Terri learned early in starting ARF.

But Mid-West Metal picks up the phone first sometimes, too. With the urging of Steven and Brenda, the company was instrumental in securing ARF assistance from places like Pet Smart back when a flood threatened to sink everything Terri had worked so hard to build.

In the end, both acknowledged, there is no doubt that Terri is ARF's biggest asset.

"She's got that total package, and she's very appreciative," Brenda said. "Believe me, there are tons of people who would like to be in her position."

"She's got one of those contagious smiles," Steven continued, "and you always get the big hug."

"We love her," Brenda added.

Steven nodded. "Who doesn't?"

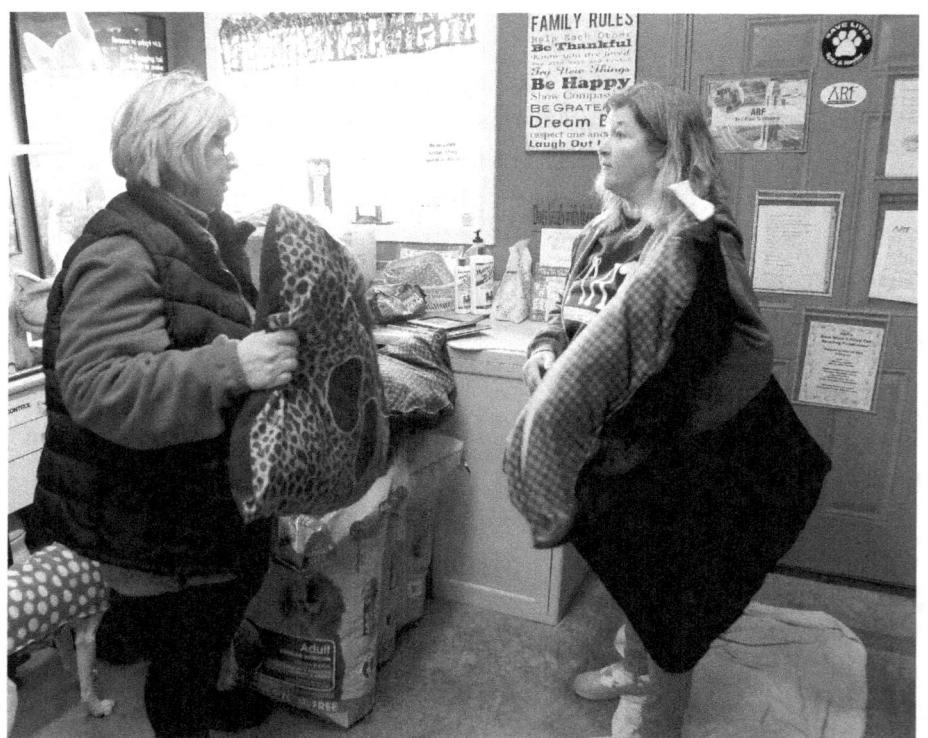

Terri and Dana Salkoski work with bulky bedding in the Catty Shack.

Cat Woman

"Are you the cat woman?"

"Yes, I am," Dana Salkoski answered with her characteristic laugh. "For better or worse."

Holder of a college marketing degree, she was a woman who had been working with special-needs children, and was also active as a volunteer with a nearby city's animal shelter when she finally went to work for it. The place was far from a wholesale killing shelter, she said, but it did happen there sometimes.

In working with the animals there, however, even that began to weigh on her.

"There came a point where I needed to switch directions," she said, and having encountered Terri and ARF in the course of her work, she threw her lot in with theirs, a job that now also includes grant-writing.

As the person in charge of ARF's cat population, which numbered about 75 when this was being written (a figure she acknowledged was smaller than usual) she does everything for them. That includes checking them in, vaccinating them, examining them for ringworm, having them spayed and neutered and facilitating their adoptions. But while adoptions run in cycles, with January and August being typically busy months, it's not unusual for some cats to spend years at ARF. In fact, given the cat house's homelike atmosphere, those felines seem perfectly content to live out their lives there.

Walk inside and it truly seems like more of a home atmosphere, with satisfied cats languidly lounging about, including on pillows horizontally mounted on a bare tree that seems to be growing from the middle of the living room floor. There are a couple friendly little black dogs, too, and one other grateful resident.

"Want to see Wilbur?" Dana asked, before leading a visitor to a hallway where the pinkish-white porker seemed happy to be resting on the floor, magnificent in his, uh, pigginess.

Anyway, lengthy stays just naturally lead to heightened familiarity.

"I really know every cat," Dana said, adding her job includes monitoring their behavior around the other cats.

The owner of four cats herself, and a woman who has fostered many others, she took a look through ARF's cat data base to come up with some memorable ones to talk about.

There was the cat that came in with the bone of its nose exposed, a cat that, perhaps in honor of Terri's husband, Jose, Dana's husband, Todd, named Njose.

There was the cat they thought had a broken jaw, but it turned out to just be a loose flap of ripped skin. Its name? "We called him George Foreman," Dana said, "because he took one on the chin."

Then there was Pinny, so named because her owner's wacky – or dare we say, stupid? - sense of fashion dictated that, before being taken to ARF, she have the cat's ears pierced with safety pins.

Then there was Audrey One, as differentiated from Audrey Two, who came to ARF as a newborn, born at a local home improvement center, and has remained there the entire nine years since.

"She has a little entourage that hangs out with her," Dana said.

Yet another memorable ARF cat was Maggy, little more than a kitten, whose head was totally ripped open in back, and who was non-responsive while maggots festered in her wound.

Back at ARF, people wondered what they were going to do with the little thing.

"Terri said, 'We're going to do whatever we can,'" Dana recalled, remembering how they worked diligently with tweezers, picking maggots out of Maggy's head.

True to ARF's mission, Maggy began to thrive, receiving medical care and attention that included playing with hats and wigs.

"She was such a character!" Dana recalled, adding that the cat knew real love and as good a life as it was possible for her to have in the four months before she died.

It's that kind of effort that makes Dana so proud to work for this organization.

"I don't know what I'd do if we didn't have ARF and I couldn't see all the kitties," she said.

Guess Who's Coming to Dinner?

Animals come into Terri's life at all hours of the day. For example, she and Jose were sitting around relaxing with guests invited over for dinner when a new ARF arrival – a three-day-old pygmy goat – was delivered to their door.

"She's tiny, tiny, tiny" Terri marveled, discussing the sweet little goat.

Word was, when it had been rejected by its mother, it was sold to a young lady who quickly discovered that raising a goat was not going to be the bag of laughs she anticipated it would be. After all, the little thing had to be bottle-fed every two-and-half hours, and was suffering from what seemed like diarrhea, though Terri explained that at this stage in its life, it was a natural process. The young lady who had brought it to ARF, by the way, had diapered it.

Anyway, the doorbell rang, and there was an ARF volunteer and the little white goat, complete with a black eyepatch and rubbery pink hooves.

"She looked like a little squeaky toy," Terri said, at least until she began bawling "maaaaaa … maaaaaa …"

To say the least, its arrival created quite a stir among her dinner guests.

"My friends were just in disbelief," Terri said, noting this firsthand experience served them a taste of what her life as a dedicated animal rescuer truly entails, of what, indeed, is commonplace.

Anyway, ARF happily took on the busy feeding schedule for the little goat, which was named Flora, and it will undoubtedly happily thrive until, in the end, it finds a safe, full-time home. Of course, that's exactly what the young lady apparently wanted in the first place.

When she turned over Flora to an ARF worker in the parking lot at Central High School, she also gave that worker a blanket, a bottle and a book on how to raise baby goats, Terri said.

A potential adopter gets to know an ARF cat.

Chupacabra

Chupacabra, the Mexican Bigfoot, is alive and well and living in Terri Panszi's closet! Well, OK, it's actually Chupacabra the cat, that's alive and well and living in Terri's closet.

How it got in there was, Terri's son Cody was working as a counselor at Muncie's Youth Opportunity Center, saving money for a move out West, when he spotted a stray black cat. Being his mother's son, he thought the kids he was in charge of could learn important lessons of responsibility and kindness by caring for it.

But what would they name it?

"Tim Allen!" hollered one young fan of the old "Tool Time" star.

That won't work, Cody told him, because the cat's a girl.

"Miss Tim Allen!" hollered the same kid, who was apparently not one to give up easily.

In the end, Chupacabra was the name chosen.

Unlike most Bigfoot-type creatures, however, this cat had totally had it with the wild, outdoor life.

"She *did* her time outside," Terri said. "She loves being inside now. She wants no part of being outside."

Anyway, when Cody left the YOC, he took Chupacabra with him, figuring she might not have that great a life with the teenage boys in the YOC residence hall. Taken to his Mom's house, the cat set up a comfortable, even luxurious residence, in Terri's closet.

"Her bed's in there," she said. "Her litter box is in there. Her food and water are in there."

And Chupacabra is in there, too, though when Terri walks past, a black curling leg and paw occasionally appears, as if motioning her inside for a visit.

"She's welcome to come out," Terri added, "but no, no ..."

Foundation of Support

When you are running a non-profit like ARF, money is always an issue. So it was that Terri hoped to become a part of the locally prestigious Community Foundation of Muncie and Delaware County's funding circle. As anyone knows, though, these things can take time. When ARF tried to secure funding to fence its newly developed five-acre Bark Park, Terri was asked what she would do if the thing proved to be a flop.

"Then we'll roll up the fence and bring it back to you," she jokingly replied, but that facetious assurance didn't loosen the purse strings, either.

She came to understand that what she needed to do was to offer some example of ARF's benefits, and do it in an unforgettable way. Happily, it was about this time Kathryn Kennison gave her an excellent opportunity to do so.

As director of BSU's E.B. and Bertha C. Ball Center, Kathryn set Terri up with a speaking engagement, one in which the ARF founder brought some orphaned kittens and asked if anyone in the audience wanted to feed them.

Indeed, they did, as hands shot up.

"I handed everybody a blanket with a kitten in it," Terri remembered, noting how the crowd reveled in the chance to have meaningful encounters with the tiny, helpless creatures. Among the audience members, apparently, were some who got back to the Community Foundation, expressing how interesting and worthwhile Terri's presentation had been.

It wasn't long before her phone rang and a Community Foundation official told her one of Terri's audience members had declared she wanted to start an endowment for ARF.

As it turned out, that audience member was Patricia Schaefer, the daughter of a late Hoosier industrialist, and to say the least, she had been very impressed by the feeding of the kittens.

In fact, she was impressed to the tune of $100,000.

Through the Community Foundation she started ARF's endowment with that amount, the largest Pat, who now has an ARF dog herself, had ever given.

"She's the sweetest, sweetest thing," Terri said of her very generous benefactor.

Since that time, by the way, ARF has benefitted greatly from the kindness of the Community Foundation, receiving a number of grants and even personal donations from its vice-president, Suzanne Kadinger.

"I don't know what we'd do without them," Terri said.

A Thanksgiving Feast

There was a time when people who didn't spay and neuter their pets were a personal affront to Terri, but then she met a lady named May who owned the canine parents of Senor Rubio and Emilita, two nice ARF chihuahuas, and learned a personal lesson.

The woman in question was elderly and poor, living in a two-room rental off Madison Street.

"This lady's dogs had puppies all the time," Terri recalled. "We even gave her vouchers to get them both fixed, but she never told us she had no transportation."

Her dogs' hyperactive reproductive activities notwithstanding, the ARF folks grew to love May from visiting her to pick up the new generations of puppies her dogs seemed to be constantly creating.

"She loved her dogs," Terri said, noting how May would frequently call ARF to see how her puppies were faring there. "Her home was so tiny, but everything done in that house was done for the comfort of her dogs."

It was during a house visit on the cusp of Thanksgiving that the woman proudly told Terri of her plan to celebrate the upcoming holiday, which she had prepared for by walking to an Aldi's market down the street with her hard-saved money in her purse.

"And we're going to have chicken breasts!" May proudly revealed, as if talking about caviar and truffles, noting that she had bought three breasts, one for her male dog, one for her female dog and one for her.

That exchange stuck in Terri's mind as she considered May's circumstances, her humble home and the rickety little fenced area she had cobbled together in her backyard for her dogs to play inside. When Thanksgiving Day finally arrived, Terri just had to act.

Assembling her family's bountiful leftovers, she enlisted Cody's help and drove to May's house with what must have seemed a literal feast to the elderly woman.

"She was thrilled out of her mind," Terri recalled. "It made her day."

What finally happened to May? Terri doesn't know. Not long afterward she went by her house and the little fenced area May had built was gone, and so was she.

Still, it had been a meaningful Thanksgiving encounter, perhaps especially for Cody, who learned something about helping others and told her, "Mom, I'm so glad we did that."

What's more, Terri learned a lesson, too.

"What May taught me was, it's not bad people that have puppies," she said. "I like the wisdom that comes with age. I really do."

Meeting a special cat brings a smile to a woman's face.

Herbert

Far, far, far from being a gullible person, Kathryn Kennison is wise to the ways of the world. A skilled writer and the driving force behind Ball State University's popular, annual Magna cum Murder mystery writing convention, which was held for years in Muncie before moving to Indianapolis, she is also director of the university's E.B. and Bertha C. Ball Center.

On a personal note, she also has loads of chutzpah, and a lot on the proverbial ball.

You can pretty well figure Kathryn is joking, then, when she calls Terri "evil and manipulative" for the way she hooked her up with a special-needs cat named Herbert.

At least, she's joking to a point …

This happened one lovely September day when the Ball center director, who already had six or seven cats back home, paid a visit to ARF's Catty Shack, as she occasionally did, just to pass time with some other felines. She was immediately struck by a kitten in a carrier, one whose head was nearly as big as its body, the result of being hydrocephalic.

"He would tip over in his carrier," Kathryn recalled, speaking from her office, a busy looking, book-lined place where the volume and variety of reading material hint at her wide range of interests, literary and otherwise.

Feeling affinity for the poor little black-and-gray striped kitten with the white belly, she took Herbert from his carrier, petted him and also felt an instant connection. In no time she was intent on calling her husband, Dick, about bringing the sweet little thing home.

That's when Terri piped up.

"Oh, Kathryn," she assured her, "you don't need to call Dick about the kitten. I know you'll bring him back."

Just like that, probably even Kathryn realized the hook had been set. Driving Herbert home, she pulled into the driveway as Dick, a retired United States Air Force officer, was pulling out. Placed on the ground, the kitten began happily batting at crabapples.

"What is that?" Dick gruffly demanded, leading Kathryn to reveal the obvious.

"It's a cat."

"What's wrong with it?" he asked, and was told.

"Well, you take that cat back to ARF," were his final words.

Fortunately for Herbert, Kathryn's final words, spoken in her mind, were, "I think we're gonna have to keep him."

When Dick returned, he noticed the addition of a tiny litter box that had been placed in their home by his wife, who showed she shared a devious streak with Terri by then placing the kitten in her husband's lap, whereupon it began to purr. Whether or not Dick realized it at the time, Herbert was home.

While the conventional wisdom was that Herbert's condition meant he wasn't long for this world, he lived more than six years, making a wonderful impression on the Kennisons during that time.

"He was just a good cat," Kathryn recalled, "and smart as he could be. He was a delightful cat."

While Herbert's forehead remained misshapen as a result of his medical condition, his body eventually caught up with his head's size. At one point, his eyelids were operated on by Dr. John Boyce, work necessitated to keep his lids from scratching his eyes.

What sort of procedure was that?

"Whatever Zsa Zsa Gabor had done about 40 times," Kathryn answered.

Anyway, in the end, she was perfectly happy that Terri had used psychology, her womanly wiles and maybe even a devious streak to facilitate her adoption of Herbert.

"She is shameless when it comes to finding homes and taking care of her babies," Kathryn pronounced.

And that's just fine with her.

Oops

Once upon a time when she volunteered as a worker at the Muncie Animal Shelter, Terri took on a dog named Sparky. "He was a little, blond, scraggly guy," she said, and only about six or seven weeks old, and her heart went out to him because in the big kennel in which he was kept, the larger puppies bullied him. This was a few years ago, her now-adult son Cody being a kindergartener back then, and for Mother's Day, Jose had just bought her a pair of fancy diamond earrings.

Having longer locks back then, there came a time that she was bent over inside the kennel to grab Sparky and take him home, when a bigger puppy bit at her hair. Then, much to her surprise and consternation, it also pulled off one of her new diamond earrings.

"I turned in time to see him go gulp," Terri recalled. Sure enough, the little rascal had swallowed it.

The first thing she did was go to shelter superintendent Gayle Workman with what must have seemed an odd request: Save that puppy's poop. The second thing she did was head home to Jose with what, for him, was one of those bad news and even "badder" news deals.

The bad news was, "I've brought home a new puppy."

The "badder" news was, "And another puppy ate my earring."

Soon adding to this tale of woe was the fact that Sparky developed Parvo, which the Panszis cured at a cost of about a thousand bucks. Then Sparky fell out of their house's loft, a tumble he survived with the addition of more veterinarian payments. What's more, Sparky soon developed a nasty temper and became a threat to bite people, resulting in the forced extraction of his teeth.

But enough of the fun stuff … let's get back to the other puppy's poop, which Gayle had been dutifully collecting.

"I went through it with a fork, chopping it up, trying to find my earring," Terri recalled, "but I never did."

Anyway, that earring was the last diamond Jose ever gave her.

"He says my dogs are my diamonds," she explained with a laugh that said, indeed, they are.

Terri in her place of joy, ARF's Adoption Center.

From Shelter to Safety

It was a typical winter Wednesday morning at Terri Panszi's house during the writing of this book. With a welcoming spirit, she sat at her
kitchen table near a note-taking visitor, sipping coffee, while scrolling
through ARF's Facebook page to reveal the three dogs – Cleo, Buddy

and Rain – they had just obtained from the Muncie Animal Shelter. The three dogs all had heart worm, and before ARF snagged them, the shelter had posted that it was waiving its adoption fee for them because of that sad fact.

This did not make Terri, as the old saying goes, a happy camper.

"Free is never good," she said, explaining that to her way of thinking, a certain kind of person was going to react to that enticement, and they were not necessarily people who would have those bedraggled dogs' best interests at heart. Cruel, unscrupulous people were known to use some shelter dogs as "bait" to train pit bulls to fight, after all, and she knew for a fact that sometimes adopted puppies and kittens were fed to snakes.

"It costs ARF $400 to treat heart worm, and for others it's even more than that," Terri said. "Now, what person that took a free dog is going to pay that?"

It seemed a pretty good point.

Still, at that very moment, ARF was mining its resources to treat and neuter those three dogs, as well as care for a litter of homeless puppies that had been featured on the front page of The Star Press the morning before. Cute and vulnerable as only puppies can be, they had been snagged by ARF, too.

Putting out a Facebook appeal for funds, ARF had raised $2,500 in just five hours, money that included one woman's single gift of $1,000, an amount that had taken Terri aback.

"I don't even know her," she said.

With any of that $2,500 that was left over after treating the new additions, she added, ARF intended to begin funding a "From Shelter to Safety" account for the sole goal of removing cats and dogs from animal shelters. For that possibility, she said, she had ARF's backers to thank.

"I take very seriously and gratefully their kindness and generosity," Terri said.

Raccoons

The sky was gray, a light snow was falling and, curled into a tight ball beneath the frozen shrubbery just beyond Terri's kitchen window, lay a raccoon. Nearby it, Terri had placed a plastic pet carrier stuffed with blankets that the raccoon could crawl into in the unlikely event that it chose to do so. There was also food.

"Here's your breakfast, it's OK," Terri had cooed while taking the food outside. "He had dog food on Tuesday, yesterday he had crockpot chicken and this morning he had cat food. ... And marshmallows for dessert."

So far, though, whenever she approached it, the raccoon only looked her way and growled. Nevertheless, she had reason to hope the marshmallows would eventually break the figurative, if not the literal, ice.

"Raccoons love marshmallows," Terri said.

She had acquired this important bit of raccoon wisdom from no less an expert than Diana Shaffer, the legendary local wildlife rehabilitation expert, consulting her when a family of raccoons she loved had climbed to the very top of a tall pine tree.

This had all begun when Terri adopted the litter of raccoon babies, bottle fed them, then tried to promote their return to the wild by feeding them shrimp and chunks of cod placed in plastic kiddie pools. Then one day she went out to visit her raccoons, and they were all up a tree.

"How do I get them down?" Terri asked Diana.

"Marshmallows," Diana answered.

So Terri carried out some marshmallows and, sure enough, all the raccoons came down. Unfortunately, once they had eaten the marshmallows, they all went right back up again. Still, they stayed in the area of their birth. Terri later wrote all her neighbors, asking them not to be afraid if a raccoon approached, and not to hurt it, either. It likely wasn't sick, it had simply been raised by a human being.

Those weren't the only raccoons Terri raised, either, another litter having included Leo, who she loved and lugged around and who played with toys.

"I slept with a raccoon more than once," Terri admitted. "Then he went off on his own, too. On occasion I would go out and kind of call for him, "Leo! Leo!"

But that was back then. If the raccoon under the shrubbery outside her kitchen window now ever decided to trust her, he couldn't have been in better hands. After all, Terri loves raccoons like, well, raccoons love marshmallows.

Team Players

Loving dogs and cats and caring for the welfare of the most imperiled of such creatures is all it takes to appreciate ARF, as well as for ARF to appreciate you. Combine that love with the sort of business and financial acumen required to keep a place like ARF up and running, however, and that appreciation only deepens.

Doug and Kathy White are two perfect examples. Married for 28 years, he is a First Vice President and Senior Trust Officer for First Merchants Trust Company, while she is the Chief Financial Officer of Muncie Power Products. Together they form an invaluable resource to help Terri Panszi and ARF navigate what can be some hazardous economic straits, providing wise counsel in any number of sophisticated business disciplines. In short, theirs is the sort of assistance that helps attract money.

Neither claims credit for it, though.

"It's always the community that rallies and keeps ARF from closing up," said Doug, while he thumbed through cell phone photos of their dogs on a Friday afternoon in his wife's fifth-floor office, proudly showing them to a visitor.

Less easy to quantify was another ARF benefit observed by Kathy.

"I think there's a little angel on Terri's shoulder sometimes," she said, citing as an example how ARF rallied from its devastating flood.

Besides their business skills, they flat out love dogs, and always have.

"Day I was born," Kathy confirmed.

"If you come to my house," Doug added, "you're going to end up with a dog in your lap."

Of course, it could be any one of six. Koko. Hopsy. Buttons. Jack Frost. Jill. Bandit. These little guys and gals, one a Yorkie, the others Pomeranians or variations thereof, are like their children, with Jack Frost and Jill, who came to the Whites after a perilous existence living in a farm field, being the parents of Bandit.

Longtime friends who grew up near each other, when their relationship progressed to marriage, they sat down and planned their animal family like other couples might plan for their human one. Still, their ARF involvement has made that family an extraordinarily extended one, since between adoptions and fostering, 50 ARF dogs have come through their doors. What's more, like some of ARF's most dedicated volunteers, they have favored elderly and special-needs animals.

From the very start, neither was under any delusions about what peculiar challenges assisting an animal rescue organization might entail. For example, after Kathy was first asked to prepare ARF's financial statements, she was given a bag of receipts to go through.

"And a couple cats had peed on it," she noted, with sort of a smile. "They'd peed on the receipts, too."

Their involvement goes back to ARF's earliest days when, as neighbors of Terri's, they would actually meet in their yards, using the opportunity to snatch a quick smoke before they all quit cigarettes. By the time their initial stints were over, they had been on the board a dozen years.

"We actually implemented term limits to get rid of ourselves," Doug admitted with a laugh.

These days, he is an ARF consultant in fundraising and such, while Kathy is back on the board. Meanwhile, both have held other ARF offices, as well as taken an active role in many other local charities and organizations.

In discussing adoptions, Kathy proves she is wise to the ways of animals and their ability to tug at one's heartstrings.

"Quite frankly, the animals pick you," she said, recalling how she met Mia, some breeder's neglected Pomeranian castoff that became one of her soul dogs. "It was obvious. I just knew she had picked us."

For that reason, she added, she is leery of going to ARF these days.

"I'm scared to death to visit," she said, chuckling, "because when I do, I have another dog or cat."

At least their house is always ready for a new arrival, though. They remodeled it with an eye toward doggy comfort and safety, from the little fence around their pool to the nicely heated, cooled and lighted dog room inside.

Not that the Whites are always there with their dogs to enjoy it, however. Once a year they journey to Italy, where Kathy's job takes her on professional business, and on their most recent voyage they took along Bandit ... well, sort of. You know those Internet features where somebody mounts someone's image on a stick and a piece of cardboard, calls it "flat Willy" or "flat Mabel" or "flat Whoever" and takes pictures of it in exotic locales?

Well, the Whites did that with "flat Bandit." Consequently, they have a picture of their little dog – or, at least, his face - visiting the Vatican, complete with a member of the Swiss Guard standing behind at attention. Pretty impressive, especially for a dog.

The Tale of Dusty Tater

Doug White wrote this account of adopting a favorite dog.

In the many years since joining the ARF board, Kathy and I have fostered and/or adopted 50 dogs. One such little guy was a Terrier mix we named Dusty Tater. He was the sweetest, but most unusual looking little guy. To us he was an absolute treasure with beautiful eyes. Dusty came to ARF after a telephone complaint from a lady who lived on a busy road southwest of Muncie. She said that he supposedly belonged to a neighbor; however, he spent many nights running loose and was usually found in the fenced-in dog run behind her house with her Rottweiler. Apparently he was small enough that he could tunnel under the fence and cuddle up with her big dog for warmth. He was also very underweight with little fur, so she began feeding him. After several months of this she decided enough was enough and she called ARF.

He was brought to the ARF sanctuary house and put in a witness protection program of sorts, in case his very neglectful owners showed up to claim him. As soon as Dusty came to ARF, Terri thought of us and asked us to come by and see him. We went over to ARF promptly and decided after just a few minutes that he could come to our house as a foster dog and that we would help ARF find him a forever home.

Well, right off the bat Dusty became an instant hit in our home and neighborhood. We began taking him on regular walks. One time, right after he came to stay, a well-meaning neighbor told me that he looked like an opossum. I, of course, took offense and denied the assertion, but he did look a bit like one. Anyway, in our minds he was very handsome!

About a week or so after we began to foster him a lady from Union City, Ohio said she might like to adopt him. I decided I wanted to be the one to take him over for a visit and inspect her house for suitability. As it turned out the house was fine, but the lady wasn't sure about Dusty and said she wanted to think about it. When I got back in the car with him for the journey home I began to cry. That's when I realized that I wanted this dog. We adopted him later that day. After a few months he was no longer underweight and his coat came in beautifully.

One thing I haven't mentioned before about Dusty is that he was a bit of a darter and he would sometimes run off if he saw an open door. In one such instance, our housekeeper Missy was at the house cleaning. For some reason she opened the front door and Dusty ran out. Missy loved animals and was not about to let Dusty run away on her watch, so she ran out the door after him. A fairly serious thunderstorm was fast approaching and she was bound and determined to get him back in the house before it really hit. Dusty headed out of our neighborhood and onto busy Moore Road with Missy running as fast as she could right behind him.

As luck would have it, and I am certain God's help, Terri Panszi was on her way home in the ARF van and was headed straight toward Dusty and Missy in the opposite direction. As soon as Terri realized what was happening she stopped the van and was able to assist Missy in catching Dusty. They all got home safe and sound, albeit very wet. In time, Dusty became a perfect member of our dog pack and had a wonderful life with us.

Cancer took him from us very quickly about 8 years after we adopted him. We will always remember that great little dog and those fantastic, beautiful, friendly eyes. We love you still, Dusty Tater.

ARF's Nikki Kirby introduces a BSU volunteer to his work.

Nikki and Hazel

It was an early winter afternoon, and the ARF Adoption Center's office was humming with activity. While cacophonous barking rang from the back, co-director Jane Schowe edged past her crowded desk in search of some timely and essential paperwork, with warmly bundled volunteers walking in and out. The room's walls were covered with animal-related decorations, like a sign proclaiming "My Dog Is My Heart," plus assorted official notices. The office's floor space was at a premium, too, with a large cage and a padded rest station sitting empty while two sweet, muscular pit bulls ambled over for sniffs and rubs behind their ears. Into this busy mix came Nikki Kirby, wearing a bright pink ARF shirt, looking rushed.

"I became a vegetarian a month after I started working here," she said, explaining that she had hit the drive-through at a Burger King back in those college days, took one bite from the chicken sandwich she had ordered, then thought, forget it.

Before this interview, Terri had predicted two things: Nikki would talk about her dog Hazel, and she would cry. Sure enough, one minute into the interview, Nikki said, "You probably want me to talk about Hazel." Then her voice had cracked as she added, "I may have to email you."

OK, that would be fine. Still, she could talk about this place and her job.

What was her title? "I don't know what it would be," she answered, though she is clearly one of ARF's go-getters and a valuable aide to Terri.

How did she feel about ARF? "I don't wake up in the morning saying, 'Oh, I have to go to work.' It's my second home."

A Ball State University student and ardent animal lover when she first came here in 2005, she faced a learning curve like anyone else does.

"I can remember the first time Terri left me in charge," Nikki said with a grin, her long blonde hair falling over the shoulders of her winter jacket. "The rule was, don't take in any dogs."

Sure enough, then somebody arrived with a cute cocker spaniel mix that desperately needed a home, and she was powerless to help herself. Later, she was worried what Terri would say when she found out, but she needn't have been.

"She just laughed, gave the dog a kiss and said, 'Welcome to ARF,'" Nikki recalled.

That same sort of spirit is what connected Nikki with Hazel, a little tannish-brown mutt whose owners had simply abandoned when they moved out of a home near Prairie Creek Lake.

As she predicted she would need to, Nikki captured her thoughts about this on email.

"To me she was my heart dog," she wrote. "That once in a lifetime (if you're lucky) dog that makes you cry every time you think about her not being here, but for whom you would do it all over again because the pain you feel now is so overshadowed by the love you felt - and still feel – knowing that she was yours and you were hers."

When Nikki encountered Hazel, it was during her first ARF rescue trip.

"Yes, yes, an emphatic yes!" she wrote, describing her reaction when asked if she wanted to tag along. What's more, on an earlier visit to try and rescue her, the little dog had steadfastly refused to budge. This time, when Nikki called her, Hazel happily leapt all over her, apparently realizing she had found her heart human.

"I took this as a sign," Nikki wrote, adding she named the little dog Hazel because of the color of her fur and eyes, and because her favorite band is Sister Hazel. They were together 11 happy years before kidney failure claimed her.

"It's been three years," Nikki wrote, "and I love her as much now as I did when I first met her and took her home. She makes me believe in the saying, 'If there are no dogs in heaven, then I want to go where they go.'"

Since then, by the way, Nikki has married Chris Kirby, a Muncie policeman who has proved himself an invaluable companion and assistant in ARF's rescue activities. They now have a son, Quinn, who is more than three years old and seems to be following his Mom's path in life.

"I don't eat meat," he told her, proudly. "*Dinosaurs* eat meat."

Jelly, by the way, is the name of one of the pit bulls who were lounging in the office this day, and is a favorite of Quinn's. When on the way to ARF, he always asks his Mom, "Are we going to Jelly's house?"

Nikki also makes no bones about Terri being her mentor, to the point where she has started her own animal rescue center – Daisy Mae Pet Rescue (daisymaepetrescue@gmail.com) out of her home.

"I swear, Terri's an animal pusher," she joked, but with the utmost respect, citing her friend's ability to find fine homes for needy dogs and cats.

By the same token, Nikki vows to remain active with ARF, even as her own animal rescue center grows.

"I don't ever foresee quitting ARF. Terri and I call it the Hotel California," she said, referring to those haunting lyrics of that classic hit by The Eagles about checking out anytime you like, "but you can never leave."

What a Great Deal!

Walk into the ARF Thrift Market, which operates out of an old brick house on the east side of Yorktown, and what you'll find are some great deals, plus Gayle Workman, the latter sitting behind a table in front of a fireplace from which an American flag hangs. What you won't find – not anymore, anyway – are kittens and puppies.

At least, not real ones.

Back when this place used to be called the Meow 'n Mutt Market, the occasional ill-informed or devious visitor would drop off litters of young animals, perhaps somehow unaware that this place was a store.

"They thought it was, like, a shelter," explained Gayle, who insisted on the name change to help bring that practice to a halt.

When it comes to this place, Gayle, whose looks belie his age, which is 74, is indisputably the man in charge, having voluntarily run the thrift store for Terri Panszi about eight years now. Before that, through the terms served by nine consecutive Muncie mayors, he supervised the city's animal shelter over a course of about 42 years.

That means Gayle, as you will undoubtedly remember, was the guy running the shelter when, as a teenager, Terri began bringing treats to the animals inside it. He was also the guy running it when, at age 35, she finally worked up the courage to step inside it, a few steps that literally changed her life. You might surmise, as well, that as a rule, animal shelter managers – at least, at kill shelters - are not automatically high on Terri's list of favorite people. That she likes Gayle, and worked with him then, and works with him now, and that *he* works with *her* now, says something about the strangeness of life, and the loving nature of them both.

"I'm blessed," he said. "I have a lot of fun here. I meet a lot of people."

Walk past the front door of this place and you are struck by its neatness, and the variety of items for sale. There is clothing, some of it brand new and some emblazoned with the ARF logo. There is wall art, much of it trending toward the animal-related, though you can't help but notice a nicely framed, well-known reproduction of a painting of the Bard – old Billy Shakespeare himself – that would grace any writer's office. Two small baskets near the checkout counter are filled with Kit Kat candy bars, Reese's Peanut Butter Cups and, most tempting of all, some dog-bone shaped chocolates that Lowery's Candies supplies ARF, hefty little bars of deliciousness selling for just $2 apiece. There is jewelry, too, ARF license plates and a fine selection of animal-related greeting cards that were donated by a businessman.

"He even gave us the card rack," Gayle noted, while the religious music he favors wafted softly from a nearby radio.

Looking back on his municipal career, he expresses a measure of pride, both for his longevity, plus the fact he did the very best he could, and maybe some regret, too.

"The city never wanted to give us *nothing*," he complained, adding that when Terri asked him to take over the thrift store, he accepted on one condition. "I said, 'You leave me alone. Let me run it.'"

With that guaranteed, he scrubbed it and restored it, noting, "If you'd walked in when I walked in that first day, you'd have said, 'Oh, God.'" These days, he faithfully staffs it weekdays from 9:30 a.m. to 4 p.m., brings the previous week's deposits to ARF every Monday, and loves who he works for.

"Listen,'" he said, citing Terri and ARF for the help they gave him back in the day at the city animal shelter, while other groups did nothing, or worse than nothing. "The other bunch, all they wanted to do was fight each other. Terri has helped many, many animals. She has saved many animals. We need more Terris."

Just then, a rather fetching Meow Mix clock on the wall reminded a visitor that it was time to leave, signaling the hour by playing that sing-songy Meow Mix cat food jingle, the one that goes "meow, meow, meow, meow, meow, meow, meow, meow, meow, meow, meow, meow…"

Well, you get the picture.

As for how long Gayle will remain here running the thrift shop, that's up in the air. Whether he offered it intentionally or not, though, he answered with as witty a reply as any ARF volunteer could possibly have given to that question.

"I'll be here," he said, "as long as the good Lord says, 'Stay!'"

Oso

High on a wall in Terri and Jose's house hangs a large, striking painting, a sort of cartoonish rendering of a hefty black dog, and in the dreamlike bubble hovering above his head is this: a loaf of French bread.

The portrait is by Muncie's Brian Blair, a talented artist better known for his extraordinarily scary Halloween creations, plus the large animal head shots that decorate ARF's sky-blue fence. The dog on the Panszis' wall is Oso. And the bread? That, it seems, is what made Oso's life worth living.

"His favorite thing on the face of the earth was French bread," Terri recalled with a fond chuckle "He'd choose French bread over steak."

Oso, which is Spanish for bear, was a Rottweiler, and Jose's heart dog. The little thing showed up at ARF when he was just one day old, part of a litter of six, of which only two had survived a traumatic birth after a puppy became stuck in its mother's birth canal. The woman who brought the two puppies in made an immediate unfavorable impression by telling Terri her husband was going to shoot the mother.

"*What?*" Terri said, offering to immediately go fetch that dog.

"Oh, no," the woman answered, as if everything would be all right, declining the offer of help. "My husband's a good shot."

That, of course, was the last thing Terri wanted to hear, but she quickly set about helping the two puppies. Before long, the second puppy died. With only one left, Terri and Jose began working shifts to bottle-feed the tiny fella, and against all odds, he survived. Meanwhile, Jose was falling for the tyke.

"He had already started forming that bond with him," Terri said. "With his help, Oso unbelievably made it from one day old."

She also explained why chances are excellent you've never heard of, nor will ever hear of, The French Bread Diet, which the dog followed religiously.

"Oso was *gigantic*," she said. "He weighed 190 pounds when he passed."

That was nine years after he entered their lives, however, a period of time when Oso and the Panszis had an unbelievably close connection, one Terri described as "sort of a Timmy-Lassie" thing."

"He was like our child," she recalled, noting how back then she took to carrying around a baby-bottle bag for him. "He would go, like, 'Woh! Woh!, then he'd lie down, take the bottle between his paws and drink it.'"

One time, during an office visit, Oso even did that in front of Dr. John Boyce.

"He said, 'Are you kidding me?'" Terri remembered, noting his tone conveyed the fact he was not favorably impressed by this act of doggy indulgence. "So I had to wean him off his bottle."

It was after Oso died that Brian painted the Panszis the portrait, French bread and all.

"He gave us almost nine years of good," Terri said. "He was a really good boy."

Still, after he passed, the Panszis decided to swear off keeping large dogs at home, recalling how Oso's mere bulky presence tended to make some folks nervous. Their resolve lasted about two whole months, at which point they adopted their dog Beebee who, to say the least, is no shrimp.

The ever-popular Wilbur, a resident of ARF's Catty Shack.

Little, and Not So Little, Piggies

ARF may specialize in rescuing dogs and cats, but at least four pigs have made their way there, too, including three who now call it home. The first one was Quigley.

"Cell phones were pretty new then," Terri recalled, "and we got a call from a woman who had seen a little pig fall off the back of a farm truck. But *our* story was, he had jumped."

This was in ARF's earliest days, when Terri had taken over Dr. John Boyce's former clinic on Wheeling Avenue. Having rushed the piglet to the good veterinarian for treatment of a broken ankle, she then took him home with her, learning something about the shrillness of a pig's squeal in the process.

Anyway, to say Quigley had landed in an idyllic situation didn't do his circumstances justice. In Terri, he had found a caretaker who would feed him entire boxes of tasty human cereal, and whose connection with a certain magnificent local bakery soon had him packing on what eventually amounted to about 900 pounds of pig.

"Part of that hugeness was from my dear friends at Concannon's," Terri explained, citing that magical place where, at the end of the day, their leftover crème-filled sticks, blueberry doughnuts and other delights fell on Quigley like super-sweet manna from Hog Heaven. Long before then, of course, the pig had been removed from her home to the comforting confines of ARF.

Even there, however, the evidence of Terri's feelings was obvious. As a woman who wears lipstick every day, her crimson lip-shaped smudges regularly showed up on Quigley's pale piggy skin.

As for him ...

"Whenever he gave kisses back," Terri said, "he would leave a round mud ring on my face."

Obviously, with evidence like that, there was no denying their rendezvous to Jose.

"He would say, 'You've been kissing that pig again,'" Terri recalled.

Another great memory of Quigley, she added, was his proclivity for eating cheap Dum-Dum suckers. He *craved* Dum-Dum suckers. When school kids came to visit ARF, they would feed the suckers to Quigley, who would devour the crunchy candy end then, with a pointed *pfffffft*, expertly spit out the stick.

"The kids loved that!" Terri said.

One lesson Terri took away from their special relationship was this: When it comes to food, "Pigs will eat and eat and eat and eat and eat and eat and ..."

While he's no Quigley, Chet is hardly underfed. An ARF resident for seven years, he came in as a stray, having been spotted walking around a mobile home park. Meanwhile, two other hogs living at ARF now are Wilbur, whose name is a nod to the late legendary writer E.B. White's beloved literary pig from "Charlotte's Web," and Lucy. Both pigs of the pot-bellied variety, they were only months old at the time of this writing, and weighed in at about 30 pounds each. What's more, Terri said, ARF was committed to keeping them at a manageable size.

Even though their lives at ARF aren't the food fests that Quigley enjoyed, Terri has no doubt they are content with their stays.

Being a female, Lucy is frequently adorned with a pink ribbon to differentiate her from Wilbur, and boasts one other fetchingly girlish attribute.

"She has the longest eye lashes you've ever seen," Terri said.

As for Wilbur, who came to ARF when he was the size of a kitten, he seems to be sublimely happy with his home in the Catty Shack.

"He loves the cats," Terri said. "He loves everything."

By the way, just in case you are wondering, in keeping with ARF's policy, even Wilbur has been, um, fixed.

"You go to ARF, you're gonna get neutered," Terri joked. "Gentlemen beware."

Jose

Ask Jose Panszi what life is like married to Terri, and by the same token, essentially married to ARF, and a thoughtful look crosses his face, along with a smile.

"It has been different," he acknowledged, noting that in the beginning of their years together, he was far from being an animal activist. "It has been an adventure. I went along. It's called love, or whatever."

Stockily-built, gray-haired and bespectacled, he was wearing a bright green ARF T-shirt under a black vest as he stood behind the bar in this, his neatly kept basement "man cave." There was music in abundance down here, including vinyl albums and compact disks. The recordings on them marked him as a man of eclectic tastes, ranging from rock to classical, with a special spot for Frank Sinatra and jazz masters like Dave Brubeck with the legendary Paul Desmond on alto sax, plus Motown and Mexican music. A tastefully decorated place, artwork based on "Don Quixote," plus other intriguing collectibles, hung on a wall or filled shelves. Lined up behind the bar, some in beautifully decorated boxes and equally impressive decanters, were bottles of remarkably good liquor, including bourbons, tequilas and mescals, the last with pale worms floating ghostlike in their clear liquid.

A sign on a wall alongside the bar, meanwhile, hilariously noted that, "In dog beers, I've only had one."

Dogs.

Becoming accustomed to Terri's great love of them and all other animals, he admitted, had taken some time.

"There are no limits for Terri, as far as animals are concerned," he said, then joked about how early on, her visual acuity, and then her total lack thereof when it came to critters in the kitchen, confounded him. "She's a woman who, at dusk, from a quarter-mile away, can see a squirrel crossing the road and yell, 'Look out!' Then we'd be in our kitchen and I'd say, 'Can't you see that *cat* sitting on the counter?'"

Apparently she couldn't, or not well enough to chase it off, anyway.

But now, Jose, who also knows his way around fine wine, loves the animals they encounter, too. That doesn't mean they get the run of his man cave, though. Apart from two-legged friends, admission down here is limited to Beebee and Anna, his two big dogs, and his cat Diego, whose presence here is barely noticeable, due to a unique litter box that is built *into* a wall. The cat enters it through a square hole cut near the floor, and exits the same way. Access to clean the litter box is through a nearby closet door. The benefit: No unpleasant clumps of you-know-what in sight down here.

Dropping a few ice cubes into a couple glasses, Jose proceeded to pour himself and a visitor drinks from a bottle of Old Rip Van Winkle bourbon, then set the bottle into the flattened palm of an upside-down plastic hand that suddenly began inching its way across his bar. Just before it was about to plunge off the edge, with his visitor about to dive in a last-ditch, heroic effort to rescue the whiskey, it stopped.

Beyond doubt, it was a pretty cool toy.

As a kid, cool toys were few and far between for Jose, whose mother was dead and whose father drove a taxi in Mexico City. What he did give his son, though, was constant encouragement to go to college and make something of himself. Jose did just that, which eventually led him to become a physician specializing in neurology.

So keep that in mind: He is a doctor, a healer. In discussing Terri, himself and ARF, he emphasizes that they are *not* business people, and ARF is not a business. Some of the expenses associated with running ARF that they have routinely dealt with, not to mention the decisions that they make for the animals' benefit, would undoubtedly give a reputable accountant nightmares. Back when Jose did it, for example, refinancing their house to get $30,000 to keep ARF afloat in its early days must have seemed like an incredibly foolhardy risk.

It worked, though, and they have both grown as a result

"Terri has become very savvy in many ways," he continued, filling a bowl with Cheetos whose fiery, south-of-the-border nature was hinted at by their crimson color and the flaming graphics on the package.

One area in which Terri is more savvy now, by the way, is personal safety. It may surprise you, or maybe it won't, but her life has been threatened before in the course of following her passion. In no way does that faze her.

"She would die saving an animal," Jose said, matter-of-factly. "I don't have any doubt. I don't have any doubt."

But now, he added, if she needs to contact the authorities about a potentially dangerous situation, she will. Thankfully, typical situations are more often inconvenient than life threatening, like the time they were heading to a funeral in Parker City and she hollered "Stop!" Having spotted a turtle crossing the road, she hurriedly picked it up and ran it into the safety of a muddy patch of woods.

Then there was the injured raccoon she picked up from a highway and took to a veterinarian, who recommended she find a shovel and bash in its head. Instead, Jose said, she took it home to their garage, taking care to leave up its door as she nursed it back to health. Sure enough, on the day it was well enough, it just wandered off.

Once, for several weeks, a little raccoon that had fallen from a tree lived in their bathroom. Another raccoon, this one big, was Nina, who loved being carried around by Terri, and would gently play with her earrings.

A woman who likes her sleep, she has nevertheless spent night after night caring for injured animals, Jose continued. When a street cat so torn up they named him Scabby arrived one day, knocking at a window to gain admittance, he more or less adopted Terri, staying until he was healthy and well fed before disappearing back on those mean streets. Scabby was no dummy.

"He knew where to come," Jose joked.

Asked to name some of his very favorite memories of her, three came quickly to mind. One was when they encountered some animal-loving youngsters who told Terri they wanted to be just like her, which didn't surprise him, but touched him deeply.

"People see the purity of Terri's heart," he said.

Another was at a local Chinese restaurant, where the Panszis encountered a sort of rough-looking woman who kept staring at Terri. Finally ambling over, she asked, "Are you Terri Panszi?" When told she was, the woman said, "I love what you are doing," and dug a ragged $5 bill from her wallet as a contribution. In other instances, he said, kids have actually held birthday parties where they have foregone presents in favor of collecting contributions for ARF.

The most amazing thing he has ever seen, however, was when Jackie Michael, who didn't even know Terri, wrote out the check that made acquiring ARF's Riggin Road facility a reality, and bought it for her.

"To me, that was, 'Wow!'" Jose recalled. "She had the vision of knowing what Terri was doing. Who *does* that?"

As Jose talks about Terri, his love for her is obvious. Equally obvious is her love for him. Of course, that's not to say their lives together have been unremittingly carefree and joyous. There was, for example, the escape of Terri's tiny heart dog Carlos under Jose's watch, while she was making a quick visit to Colorado. Fortunately, as you'll recall, folks at the Muncie Animal Shelter found the little guy and returned him – no harm, no foul, right? But even now, that memory sends a chill down Jose's back.

"Oh, *John*," he said to a visitor, shuddering, "I'm telling you. I felt so bad I thought I was gonna have a heart attack."

In fact, having previously decided to donate his body to science when the time comes, he actually found himself wondering, "Where's that number?" meaning the number to call to have the guys in white come pick up his carcass. And truth be told, when Terri recounts the story with little Carlos safely asleep on her arm, his tiny pink tongue unselfconsciously protruding from the right side of his mouth, even she admits this: Had the dog been lost forever, there may not have been enough Marriage Enrichment Encounters available in the United States of America to patch things up between them.

Just kidding, of course … maybe.

But it's other stories, like their experiences back in Mexico, that truly illustrate the bond between them.

First, you should know that Terri can't go back there again, *won't* go back there again, based on the way that many animals are treated there. But before she made that decision, the two were walking in Mexico City one day when she spotted a famished dog on the loose. Having noticed a nearby restaurant, Jose was soon inside it, ordering a steak.

What sides did he want?

None.

How did he want it cooked?

He didn't want it cooked.

By now, eyebrows were being raised, and it took some doing to convince the folks at the restaurant that he was serious, but soon that dog which Terri had stayed with was downing the finest meal of its hard, hard life.

But even more illustrative of their unique bond and partnership is when they went on vacation to Acapulco, a place where Jose thought he and Terri could actually unwind, its beaches likely absent of needy animals. Then they encountered the malnourished horses, which were rented by the hour on the beach to anybody who wanted to ride one. The first one Terri spotted burned itself into her psyche.

"She said, 'That horse has lost its soul,'" Jose recalled, and before long, he had rented every horse in the vendor's tent-like stable.

How, that vendor might well have wondered, were they going to ride so many?

"We're *not* going to ride," Jose was soon explaining to the horses' confused but grateful owner, as they began removing the saddles from the pitiful swaybacked beasts. Before long he was hoofing it down the beach himself, to a store about a mile away, where they had earlier seen apples selling for the outrageous price of a dollar each. In a short while he was back, with lots of apples, as well as an ample supply of Neosporin.

"He was really, really trying, for my sake, to do something," Terri recalled with a warm smile, her voice cracking. "He rented those horses for the whole day, so they could have a day of peace."

With the horses' saddles off, Terri and Jose gently applied Neosporin to their sores, brushed their coats and fed them apples for the day. Furthermore, Spanish being Jose's native language, he stepped in when he heard their owner trying to arrange a little double-dipping on the side, sneakily agreeing to rent them to other beach-goers.

"No!" Jose insisted. "You know these horses go nowhere for the whole day."

That act would seem extraordinary to many, and it was, but it was also just another day of being married to Terri, and one that she will never, ever forget.

"It was a beautiful thing that he did for me that day," she said.

As for Jose, after telling the story, he took a sip of bourbon behind the bar in this, his special man cave, and smiled again. Maybe it was at the taste of the liquor, but more likely he was relishing that memory from their extraordinary marriage.

"It's been a treat, to say the least," he said. "I love her."

ARF Spouses

Obviously, when it comes to ARF spouses, Jose can be considered the ultimate, having definitely had the most practice. He's not the only spouse of an ARF activist, though. Here are a few others:

Jim Schowe

Having retired from General Motors, then from Borg Warner, and now working part-time at Benson Motorcycles, Muncie's Harley-Davidson dealership, Jim is obviously a guy who likes to keep busy. To that end, he has found, ARF is rife with potential.

"Every time there's something broken, my wife calls me first," said Jim, who is married to Jane Schowe.

A big, strapping guy, he has done work for ARF including installing fences, repairing kennels, and making doors. At one point he pondered finding a place to park his tools there, but in the end, that didn't work out.

"Every time Terri's got two square inches," he joked, "she puts a dog or a cat in there."

Away from ARF, besides riding motorcycles, he enjoys woodworking and caring for the 24 acres he keeps as a nature preserve, a place with bees and houses for birds and other beautiful, natural stuff. It's a nice getaway from the phone which, because of Jane's work at ARF, rings more or less constantly, something he finds a bit confounding.

Nevertheless, they also foster lots of dogs, though not as many as they temporarily did in the wake of the flood that hit ARF a few years ago. After that watery disaster, they temporarily had 28 dogs in their house.

"You know what," Jim said, reflecting on that time when so many animals had to be evacuated due to the rising water, "there was no other choice."

Todd Salkoski

As the athletic director and administrative assistant at Shenandoah High School, Todd gets all the practice he needs keeping critters – well, at least those of the two-legged variety - in line at work, thank you very much. But what he does for his wife, Dana, and by extension, ARF, is lend a sympathetic ear.

"I try to listen to my wife when she tells me the horror stories and the things she goes through with the animals," he said, noting the heart-breaking nature of so many of their histories. "My job is just to support my wife."

That's necessary, of course, because of her intense feelings for the animals.

"She takes it all pretty personally," he said. "She's got a big heart for them, and she wears it on her sleeve most of the time."

So, we asked, has he gotten used to her bringing home critters of the four-legged variety?

"No," he said, bluntly, then laughed. "But she sneaks some home every now and again."

Gay Ellen Barrett

Trying to tabulate the number of dogs and cats Gay Ellen Barrett and her husband, Michael, have recently fostered nearly requires a calculator.

"A litter of kittens, a cat, three dogs … no, *four* dogs …" said the First Merchants banking center manager, mentally counting them off and noting that she used to keep track of them all via a computer data base.

What motivates her ARF work?

"Well, I love animals," she said, noting at one point she wanted to be a veterinarian. "I've been an animal lover all my life. Working with ARF was a natural progression for me."

Of course, another motivation is the fact that Michael is employed there.

"I never really know when I go home at night who's going to be there," Gay Ellen said. "It could be a maggoty kitten … it could be a dog he picked up off the street."

Whatever it is, she knows that ARF or her home is the right place for it, citing the example of Alex, "the wonder husky," as a perfect example. Terribly battered as a puppy, the little thing was fostered by them, then placed in a loving, secure forever home. Alex's story is the favorite of her long involvement with ARF.

"Watching it become one of the coolest dogs God ever made," she said, "just shows what the power of love can do."

Dave Ross

A prominent businessman, Dave owns an insurance-related company that deals with catastrophes, and knows what it takes to succeed. Given that, he truly appreciates what Terri has done with ARF, being aware of the chancy odds that most not-for-profits constantly battle for survival.

"I'm just in awe of what they're able to accomplish," he said. "How many rabbits can you pull out of that hat?"

It was his wife Ann Marie's involvement that put him in touch with ARF, beginning virtually at its inception. Over those years, she has brought home any number of dogs, and more will undoubtedly follow.

"I try to act like I'm annoyed, but she knows better," said Dave, a tall and distinguished-looking man, adding that other things he does for ARF include rounding up teams for its golf outing and, of course, supporting it financially.

Then there is the promotion of animal adoptions, something Ann Marie specializes in, often through contacts made with people met in her husband's business.

"If anybody is in need of a dog, she's like Radar O'Reilly," Dave said. "She has hooked up a lot of them with dogs."

And that's just great, of course, Dave being a dog lover, too, though on reflection, even he finds his present connection with the family canines occasionally disconcerting.

"We always had hunting dogs who worked for *us* for a living," he joked. "Now, I work for *them*."

Chris Kirby

For learning about ARF, Chris couldn't have chosen a better person to make the introduction than Nikki, who is now his wife of about four years.

"I barely knew of its existence prior to meeting her," he said.

Now, of course, he knows it well.

"The work that those ladies do is just tireless," he said, citing the benefits ARF provides to the animals there, as well as to the people who adopt them, and noting he numbers it among "the finest organizations in our city."

That's in no small part due to Nikki, by the way, for whom the words "ardent" and "fervent" fail to characterize her efforts.

"My wife is the hardest working person I know," Chris said. "I don't know anybody that works harder for animals than my wife does."

Chris's own career is in law enforcement. Like his father, Bill Kirby, before him, he is a Muncie policeman, a position of authority that can be a comforting presence as he lends his help to ARF.

"Inherently, I'm a protector," he explained, noting he helped shepherd an ARF delegation headed south to Henryville a couple years ago after that small Hoosier city was walloped by tornadoes.

"We just cleaned out their shelter down there," he said, noting the relief that help provided as the city struggled to overcome the ravages of the storm. Among the dogs they brought back was one the Kirbys fostered, naming her Henri, short for Henrietta, in honor of Henryville.

His personal dog preference is for older dogs, and big enough ones that he and their son, Quinn, can enjoy a little roughhousing with. As for their own dogs, there's a beagle named Lanee and a golden retriever called Fozzie Bear, so named because they were watching a Muppet movie when he was turned in to ARF.

So, given his love of dogs, does he envision himself eventually joining the police department's K-9 unit?

Maybe, under the right circumstances.

"If they could teach my golden retriever or my fat beagle to sniff dope, I would love to bring them to work every day," Chris answered with a laugh.

ARF employee Denise Ross cheerfully goes about her work.

A Day In the Life

It was a Wednesday afternoon, a nice enough day for mid-March in east-central Indiana, with the sun slowly burning off an early morning fog. Things were also heating up in ARF's Adoption Center. With a pair of scissors, Terri Panszi was snipping open individually wrapped dog treats for the animals barking in back. Meanwhile, Jane Schowe was on the phone, checking the references of someone who wanted to adopt a dog. She might call an employer. She might call a landlord, too, to make sure pets were permitted in the applicant's rental. And if the potential adopter was a Ball State University student, she would definitely be talking to that student's parents.

"I call their parents because we don't want any pets dumped when school's over," Jane explained.

By now, Nikki Kirby was outside lugging heavy bags of cat and dog food from an anonymous looking shack to where a table had been set up. Joining her, Terri began lining up boxes of dog snacks – in this case, Beneful Baked Delights.

People had already begun filing into the center on business, with one man bearing his paycheck stub from a nearby department store, applying for a spay-neuter voucher that would freely provide that surgery for his cat. In the course of talking to him, it was discovered he had a second cat that also needed the surgery. Before he left, he had been promised two vouchers.

Meanwhile, a couple interested in adopting a cat were directed back to Dana Salkoski in the Catty Shack. Another man brought in food for the dog he had just turned over to ARF, one he had adopted just a couple weeks earlier from the Muncie Animal Shelter.

"He's a wonderful dog," he told Terri, with a hint of regret, without elaborating on why things hadn't worked out.

Outside, cars began crunching across the wet gravel of the parking lot. This was one of two days each month when those in need of it, could pick up free dog and cat food for their pets.

As usual, members of ARF's part-time cleaning staff had arrived about 8 a.m. to scrub the buildings and give the place the once over.

"They go through and check everybody and make sure everybody's good," Terri said, adding they also feed the animals. Tuesdays, Wednesdays and Thursdays from 1 to 5 p.m. and Saturdays from noon to 3 p.m. are the longest spells the dogs stay in their kennels, those being ARF's adoption hours. It's 5 p.m. when ARF closes, at least, officially.

"But they never, *ever*, get out at 5 o'clock," Terri said of the volunteers, adding that at 8 p.m., a part-timer makes the last of the day's rounds, giving medicine, cleaning up for a final time and, "tucking everybody in for the night."

At this point in the day, though, that hour was still a long way off.

After an elderly couple slowly drove up, the man removed a large bag of empty cans from his car's trunk and handed them over. "Thank you so much," Terri told him sincerely, before slinging the bag into the fenced area where ARF's cans are gathered, landing with a tinny clink. "This bag is saving some lives."

When an older woman inquired about adopting a dog, the newly hired Denise Ross, who works part-time for ARF and part-time in auditing at Mutual Bank, accompanied her and the sheltie she was interested in to ARF's Bark Park. Ross had learned about ARF at a class in community leadership, and more from ARF's Facebook page.

"When that posting came across, the pieces just kind of fell into place," she said, noting her ARF work was good for her soul. "I'm an animal lover. Always have been. For me, it's fulfilling to see dogs find good homes."

A dog named Isabella had already touched her life.

"She's the sweet, timid girl by the door," Denise said, noting the dog seemed to be breaking out of its lonely shell here. "That, for me, is what it's all about. To see a dog get better."

With things well in hand, Terri had headed across town to Mid-West Metal Products in ARF's silver Dodge Ram pickup truck, fetching a crate the generous folks there had offered her. Lucy the pig, it seemed, required it, having shown a remarkable porcine proclivity for rooting up floors with her snout. Back in the Catty Shack, meanwhile, Ball State University student Hannah Yeoman was working in a rear room when a visitor hollered her name, then hollered it again.

"Sorry, I was scooping poop," she apologized with a laugh, explaining why she had been volunteering here for three years. "It's really great to see the animals that come in here, and the transformation that takes place in them. ARF never gives up on them."

While after three years Hannah's days at BSU were apparently numbered, other volunteers, it seemed, would be showing up to take her place. In fact, it was about then a car pulled onto the lot bearing two more students, Shelby Mundy and Savannah Ugarte, the former with her leg bound in a gray plastic cast, who were interested in volunteering. Having headed into the Adoption Center, they were quickly headed out again, each bearing white sheets of paper with an introduction to ARF, its rules and the necessary waivers to sign. What had brought them here?

"We wanted to get more involved," Shelby said. "I love animals."

"And I love animals," added Savannah, noting that their sorority had visited ARF earlier and been favorably impressed.

By now, Terri had returned with Lucy's new home. While the occasional straggler had wandered in for free pet food, she noted it had been a relatively light day for food pickups, not a bad thing since the supplies of cat food were running low.

"Some days we're slammed," she said, "some days are slow."

Thankfully, dog food was more abundant, but she noted they kept the doors to the supply shed tightly shut because in the past, some folks coming in for free food had become argumentative, noting their dogs preferred another brand.

With that, Terri smiled and gave her eyes kind of an "only in America" roll.

Still, all things considered, this was a good day.

"Every day is kind of the same, but different," she said. "We never know what's going to come through the door."

Two volunteers from BSU clean while Wilbur tries to stay out of the way.

John and Pamela Boyce

In the beginning, Terri was simply a regular client of Dr. John Boyce's veterinary clinic, albeit one who showed up far more frequently than most, the beloved animals she was having treated numbering in the scores. Soon enough, however, he began discounting her services, the fervor of her efforts for animals being so obvious.

"She was just a super good-hearted animal advocate," said John, a devout Mormon, plus a husband and father of six who had earned his doctorate in veterinary medicine from Michigan State University in 1982. "And she was a very good-hearted person."

Having grown up and practiced across the country, John moved to Muncie in 1987, setting up his practice on North Wheeling Avenue, a place that Terri eventually took over for ARF after he built a modern new clinic on Riggin Road.

It was relatively early in their relationship that he discovered just how seriously Terri took her animal care, when a little pig eventually christened Quiqley tumbled from a farm truck and broke its ankle. Naturally, she brought the pig to John's clinic to be set.

"I said, 'You gotta be crazy,'" he recalled of that day, but she said she wasn't kidding, or crazy, and he went ahead and set it. Sure enough, in a couple weeks the ARF pig was getting around as good as new.

That experience only prepared him for more to come, all of which culminated in the treatment of a little dog named Snickers that had been hit twice by cars. This was delicate work in which he employed borrowed orthopedic bone plates, in company with Dr. Scott Walker, to treat the little thing's injuries, an operation done under the appraising eyes of an orthopedic equipment rep.

So far, John said, that was his most memorable ARF case, one perhaps made all the more so by the fact that to this day, that little dog doesn't care much for him. Go figure.

That's fine with him, though, since he sees his ARF work as something of a mission, one he is happy to undertake

"It's kind of giving back, a little bit, for the skills that I have," he said, adding that it also gives him a chance to practice veterinary disciplines he might not otherwise often encounter. It also gives him experience dealing with all manner of dogs and cats, likely including many beset with issues that a non-rescue animal wouldn't necessarily be facing.

"There are a lot of them that didn't work out for some reason," he noted, of these helpless critters and their pre-ARF stories.

A dog lover himself, his own have included Kelsey, a husky-shepherd mix that he healed of Parvo, a dog that came for a weekend and stayed for 14 years. The Boyces now have a couple sheltie mixes named Topaz, who is nine, and Pippin, who is five. The latter was a tiny tyke, easily held in one hand, an ARF dog that Terri asked the family to look after for a couple weeks at a time when the kids were home from college for their Christmas breaks.

Trouble was, John said, those breaks came and went with Pippin still in the house, something that he repeatedly reminded Terri about.

"I'd call and she'd say, 'I got it covered, I got it covered,'" he remembered, without her specifying just what having "it covered" meant.

At this point, you might recall Nikki Kirby's comment, delivered with true love and respect, that Terri is nothing less than an "animal pusher" when she is seeking a good home for one. John's wife, Pamela, has firsthand knowledge of this, and how it works. As previously noted, it was Christmastime when Pippin came into their lives, the kids were home from school and love was in the air.

Calling about the pint-sized dog, Terri's first words to Pamela were, "Now, you can say no, but …"

Anyone who has ever come under the spell of what you might call the Panszi Effect in matters of animal adoption will recognize that at this point, Terri had pretty much won. The Boyces just didn't know it yet.

And who could blame them? It wasn't like they had never fostered more challenging puppies than this pipsqueak before, then successfully turned them back over to ARF when their duty was done. They had, including a litter of Great Dane-mastiff mixes.

"They grew *overnight*," Pamela recalled, with amazement.

So the prevailing feeling was that Pippin would be no big deal to foster, considering he looked like "a little tiny miniature Lassie." Then their daughter, Julia, got her first look at him, and it turned out that despite the vagueness of Terri's later assurances to John, she really *did* have "it covered" all along.

"Julia just screamed," Pamela said with a warm laugh, noting it was a scream of love at first sight and instant delight.

Game, set and match.

"We really didn't need any Christmas presents under the tree that year," she added, with Pippin supplying all the holiday cheer required for the festivities. What's more, finally adopting him provided a new friend for Topaz, who was lonely and grieving the loss of Kelsey, and gave Pippin a mentor.

Anyway, if you ask John, who by some definitions could be described as a man of few words, whether he will remain associated with ARF as long as he is in practice, he answers, "Sure." And if you ask if he'll do so after he retires, he answers, "I don't know."

Still, it certainly seems possible, since he and Pamela both think the world of Terri.

"She is hands down down the most generous person I know," Pamela said. "And she's always thinking about other people."

Equally impressive, and maybe a key factor in the longterm success of ARF, is this: She's also a masterful networker.

"She's the *ultimate* networker," Pamela said, noting Terri's mantra is, "What can you do for us, and what can I do for you?"

A cat with feline leukemia will spend its last days in a loving place.

"There's Always a Place."

It was in 2002 when Jann Seymour, then a political science major at Ball State University, heard about ARF and its mission to care for, and hopefully place in good homes, the endless numbers of poor dogs and cats in need of both love and friends.

"So I went out one day to walk some dogs," she said with a laugh, "and I didn't leave for four years."

As Jann recounted this, she was working in her office in Nashville, Tenn., where she heads a non-profit that assists financially strapped people with keeping their electricity on and their water from being shut off. She and her musician husband Daniel, a bass player, have lived there seven years.

What did she do for ARF?

"What *didn't* I do," she noted, brightly, explaining that her volunteer work there included everything from writing thank-you notes and answering phones to "putting cat food on paper plates." Eventually, Terri used her own money to hire her as an assistant, a job she held for a year before going on to school to train for running a non-profit herself.

Pursuing that worthy career goal, by the way, had never entered her mind before encountering Terri. So, ARF's founder was definitely a mentor?

"Absolutely," Jann answered, emphatically. "She helped show me what I could do with my life, how to do things with your whole heart. She showed me I could actually have a career that was meaningful."

Hers were inspiring words. Of course, being an ARF veteran, she knew this writer was also expecting to hear a touching animal tale or two, and she didn't disappoint.

"There was a moment I got hooked on ARF," she said, explaining it involved a little brindle pit bull named Baxter, a dog she met on her first day there.

"Baxter had been a bait dog," Jann said, meaning that he had been used as a target in training dogs to fight. "He was covered head to tail in scars, but he was so grateful to be there. I met him the first day. The second day, I went back to see Baxter. I fell totally in love with him."

In Baxter's case, ARF expedited handling of his adoption, since word was out that his former owner was plotting to steal him away from the rescue shelter.

"So it was real important to get him in a good home," Jann recalled, and that's just what the folks at ARF did. "That was one of the first times I cried at ARF, when they took him away, but they were happy tears."

Her greatest accomplishment at ARF? It's not big, she said, or maybe doesn't *sound* big, but she knows just what it was. It came after ARF took in three puppies, which were two months old or slightly older, and had been found under a concession stand at the Lions Club park in Matthews. Not only were the dogs feral, having had virtually no contact with people, but all had Parvo, too. Early on, it was determined the three – which had been named Doc, Fozzie and Jack – would likely end up living out their lives at ARF. But one special day, she got shy little Jack to cuddle with her, just *cuddle* with her, and knew the joy of helping achieve an important breakthrough in that dog's life.

For her, it reinforced the beauty of ARF.

"There's always a place for them," Jann said. "If they can make it through the door, ARF is never going to give up on them."

She also learned a lesson at ARF that still plays out in her non-profit work today, something that has sort of become her mantra. It happened when they were stretched to the limit of space with dogs. Then someone tried to bring in yet another one. We just can't take him, the ARF folks sadly explained, regretfully advising the people to take the dog to the Muncie Animal Shelter. That's just where the dog was about to be driven when they caught sight of the poor thing, which was staring at them from the plastic pet carrier into which it had been crammed.

In a flash, the ARF folks ran after the vehicle, waving down its driver.

"We'll *make* room," somebody quickly promised, and that is exactly what they did for the dog.

It was a lesson that Jann has never forgotten. In facing important decisions, she said, there is often the official thing to do.

"But there is also the *right* thing to do," she said.

It's ARF and Terri that she credits with teaching her to do the right thing.

Once horribly abused, Arlo's dignity was restored by ARF.

Arlo

The end, for Arlo, came two weeks after he had arrived at ARF. Still, they were two weeks that had brought a profound change for the better – an almost unimaginable change, really – in that poor dog's life.

It was nearly impossible to convey the ravages he had endured, as evidenced by his look and condition when found in that ditch along a lonely country road. Ashley Conti, at the time a photographer for The Star Press, had taken an early look at Arlo, and could hardly believe her eyes.

"It was just, like, the most disgusting thing I'd ever seen," she recalled. "He looked like a pile of trash."

But now, with his head erect, his gray-brown coat was clean and fluffy as he stared into the camera from a place of love and security, his left ear drooping lower than his right. Under his nose, the faint black line of his mouth curved in what one could almost imagine was an off-kilter smile. Only his eyes, black, piercing, unblinking eyes that seemed to lock onto yours, conveyed something of the abominable, ruthless treatment he had endured.

Robin Gibson, a writer for The Star Press, had taken an immediate professional interest in Arlo's story. But hers had been a keenly personal interest, too. Now, as she sat talking about him in a campus-area coffee shop called The Cup, not even trying to mask her emotions, it was obvious that time hadn't dulled her feelings for him.

Having pulled his teeth, they being hopelessly rotted, she said ARF was preparing to neuter Arlo when pre-surgery screening revealed he had suffered significant liver damage. Just days later, he took a turn for the worse.

"He just wasn't eating anymore," Robin said. "It didn't sound like he'd be around for long. I thought it was inevitable, but it was so sad."

Still, his story having captured the public's attention, he was something of a celebrity now. With Arlo stretched out on a comfortable dog bed at ARF, the public was invited to meet him.

"People were coming up," Robin recalled. "Everybody just came over to pet him."

If Arlo's failing condition seemed extra sad, considering all he had been through, it was partly because for a short while, there was a flicker of hope that he might recover from his abuse and neglect. Sitting in Terri's back yard with the dog, Robin had been shocked when Arlo actually wandered wobbly over to her.

"I thought, 'My God, he's walking!'" the journalist recalled, adding that a certain resting place in the yard, a far cry from that ditch in which he had been found lying, was Arlo's alone. "That was his spot. He just seemed so happy."

Joining them there in the yard was Ashley.

"You could tell that his mood had changed," the photographer recalled of the newly groomed dog. "And you could tell that he hadn't gotten any love before."

But as his condition continued to precipitously slip, until he became totally unresponsive, it became obvious that putting down Arlo would be a kindness, sending him off with the level of love, care and respect that only the folks at ARF could provide.

In looking back on his story now, Ashley and Robin were asked, what were their overriding thoughts?

"It was very sad that there are people out there who will treat an animal like that," said Ashley who, like Robin, loves dogs, her voice over the phone taking on a steely edge. "That's a special kind of evil right there."

Robin's thought?

"Amazement," she said, referring to Terri and ARF. "She's always ready to take on a case like this. With a sad case like this, it'd be so hard. She knows the outcome, but it's the right thing to do."

Equally amazing, Robin added, is that from such painful experience, Terri has come up with a number of special programs to help dogs and cats and the people who love them, and that ARF has been able to sustain them.

A case in point: ARLO, which stands for ARF Really Loves Oldies.

"We're trying to match senior dogs with senior people," Terri explained. "That's our way of honoring Arlo. I love it when the universe works like that. ... He had two really good weeks. It was late in his life, but he was loved."

As for Ashley, she pointedly echoed that statement.

"I think two good weeks are better than no good weeks," she said. "At least he got to pass in an environment where somebody gave a *crap* about him, as opposed to dying in that ditch."

Home

Extraordinary people are just that, extraordinary, for a reason. They have extraordinary drive, extraordinary vision, extraordinary passion, and extraordinary belief in and commitment to some cause that fills their hearts and reverberates in their very souls. It's those people who lead the way in making this world a better place for the rest of us.

Or, as the case may be, for us, our dogs and our cats.

Terri Panszi is one of those extraordinary people, though she will howl like a hound denying that fact when you confront her with it, boldly confessing her shortcomings and crediting the folks at ARF with all the good that special, special place generates.

And, truth be told, there's an extent to which that is true. In encountering people like Terri, hanging out with her, working with her, the rest of us can't help but benefit, taking on something of her spirit and compassion. If you don't believe so, just take a drive out to ARF's campus on Riggin Road and see for yourself. It's a place where the tough work of saving imperiled dogs and cats is accomplished by dedicated people with diligence, energy and even good humor.

In the years since its founding by Terri in 1998, it has overcome obstacles ranging from lack of funding to flooding and much more besides, all to thrive. While nothing is guaranteed in this world except, as the old saying goes, death and taxes, it seems reasonable to think that ARF, the Animal Rescue Fund, will continue under the care and nurturing of the folks who have taken up Terri's cause, embraced it for their own, and will continue to do so.

For the sake of all the dogs and cats that need a home, and for Terri's sake, too, let's hope so.

"I want ARF to be forever," she said with a hopeful smile, while tiny Carlos the chihuahua snoozed on her arm, a little dog without a care in the world, which was exactly as it should be. "I want my grandson to tell his friends, 'My Granny started that.'"

About the author and photographer

John W. Carlson is a former feature writer for The Star Press of Muncie, Ind., where his columns, some of which were published in the collections "Individually Wrapped" and "Nice Try," won him a Best of Gannett award, among others. Most recently the author of "Tails From Sparky's Doghouse," where he considers himself that Mt. Summit dive bar's poet laureate, his work was cited in Ray Banta's book, "More of Indiana's Laughmakers." His humorous crime stories have appeared in Red Herring, Ellery Queen and Alfred Hitchcock's mystery magazines.

Kurt Hostetler is a former photo-journalist for The Star Press of Muncie, Ind., where his work won him a Best of Gannett award, as well as honors from the Hoosier State Press Association and the Associated Press Managing Editors. He also received an Excellence in Journalism award from the American Legion for his photo work with American troops in Bosnia.